Moreton Mo~

2ᵒ

THE COURSE COMPANION
FOR
BHS STAGE TWO

THE COURSE COMPANION
FOR
BHS STAGE TWO

MAXINE CAVE

BHSSM+T

J. A. ALLEN
London

© Maxine Cave 2000
First published in Great Britain 2000
Reprinted 2002
Reprinted 2004
Reprinted 2006
Reprinted 2011

J.A. Allen
Clerkenwell House
Clerkenwell Green
London EC1R 0HT

www.allenbooks.co.uk

J.A. Allen is an imprint of Robert Hale Limited

ISBN 978-0-85131-766-3

British Library Cataloguing in Publication Data.
A catalogue record for this book is available from the British Library.

Typesetting and design by Bill Ireson
Colour photography: Bob Langrish
Illustrations by Maggie Raynor
Cover design by Nancy Lawrence
Colour separation by Tenon & Polert Colour Scanning Limited
Printed in China by Midas Printing International Limited

Contents

Introduction

This book covers the horse care and knowledge elements of the British Horse Society Stage Two examination, along with some subject matter which leads on to the BHS Stage Three. It should be used in conjunction with *The Course Companion for BHS Stage One* to ensure that all background knowledge has been covered.

It is very important that each student studies the contents of the BHS syllabus before taking any exam, as the ultimate responsibility for covering all aspects required for the exam lies with you. Each student should also realise that at each new level they should have confirmed and improved their knowledge from the level before. For example, grooming is examined at Stage One, but will be looked at again at Stage Two, together with quartering and wisping.

The practical skills outlined within the book must be developed through "hands on" experience. There is no substitute for practical work.

In the section headed "Helpful Hints and Exam Technique" I have tried to highlight areas where, as an examiner, I frequently find candidates in trouble through misinformation, lack of preparation or misunderstanding of the requirements of the examination situation.

Maxine Cave

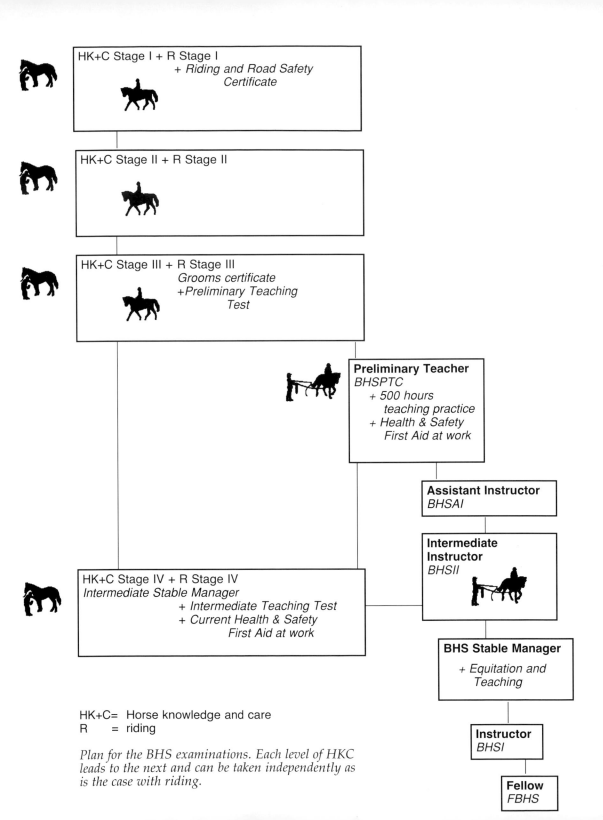

HK+C Stage I + R Stage I
+ *Riding and Road Safety*
Certificate

HK+C Stage II + R Stage II

HK+C Stage III + R Stage III
Grooms certificate
+Preliminary Teaching
Test

Preliminary Teacher
BHSPTC
+ 500 hours
teaching practice
+ Health & Safety
First Aid at work

Assistant Instructor
BHSAI

Intermediate
Instructor
BHSII

HK+C Stage IV + R Stage IV
Intermediate Stable Manager
+ Intermediate Teaching Test
+ Current Health & Safety
First Aid at work

BHS Stable Manager
+ Equitation and
Teaching

HK+C= Horse knowledge and care
R   = riding

Plan for the BHS examinations. Each level of HKC
leads to the next and can be taken independently as
is the case with riding.

Instructor
BHSI

Fellow
FBHS

1 Strapping/Grooming/ Quartering

1. Reasons for Grooming

a. To clean the horse thoroughly, which also stimulates circulation and promotes health.
b. To improve the appearance of the horse.
c. To aid the prevention of disease.
d. To help to build a relationship with the horse.

2. The Grooming Kit

a. Hoof pick – For removing packed-in dirt and stones from the hoof. Used from the heel towards the toe to prevent the point of the hoof pick accidentally digging into the frog or heels.
b. Dandy brush – For removing dry mud from the coat. Usually used on unclipped, less-sensitive parts of the body and on the legs if care is taken not to knock the bony parts of the limbs. The dandy brush should not be used on the mane and tail as it will break the hairs. Use in short, firm strokes.
c. Body brush – For removing grease and dust from the coat. Generally used on stable-kept horses, all over the body, including the mane and tail. Used more sparingly on the field-kept horse as it needs to keep the grease in its coat to protect it from the weather. Being soft, the body brush is the best one to use on the horse's face and any other sensitive areas. It is used in conjunction with the metal curry comb. When using the body brush on the nearside of the horse, hold it in your left hand, and in your right hand when on the offside. This enables you to put more strength into the slightly semi-circular movement with which the brush should be firmly applied.

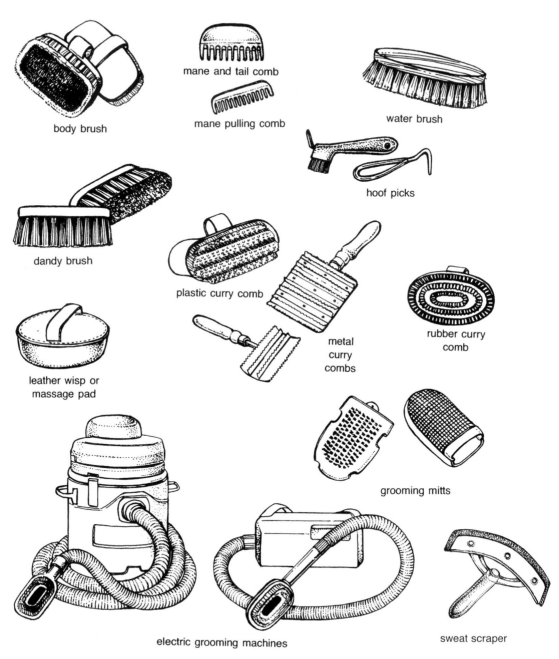

body brush

mane and tail comb

mane pulling comb

water brush

hoof picks

dandy brush

plastic curry comb

metal curry combs

rubber curry comb

leather wisp or massage pad

grooming mitts

electric grooming machines

sweat scraper

Grooming tools

d. Metal curry comb – For removing grease from the body brush. It is never used on the horse. After each stroke, the body brush should be drawn across the curry comb which is held in the opposite hand. The grease is then knocked from the curry comb by tapping it on the ground.

e. Rubber curry comb – For removing grease from the coat. Normally used on stable-kept horses, all over the body. Firmly applied in small circles, against the lie of the hair, it brings the grease to the surface.

f. Plastic curry comb – For removing mud and the loose winter coat during moulting. It is generally used on field-kept horses, all over the body. It should not be used on the mane and tail as it will break the hairs. It can be used in any kind of stroke necessary to remove the mud and loose coat. Also used to clean the body brush, it makes a good and safe substitute for the metal curry comb, especially for children.

g. Mane comb – For removing tangles from the mane. It may also be used on the tail. It is used in a simple combing action, taking a small portion of hair at a time. The smaller combs with short teeth are for mane pulling.

h. Stable rubber – For removing dust from the surface of the horse's coat after grooming. It can be used all over the horse, just like a duster.

i. Wisp/massage pad – For improving muscle tone. It can be used on muscular areas, mainly on the topline of the horse, for example on the trapezius muscle of the neck and the muscles of the hindquarters. It is used in conjunction with a stable rubber. The horse should be able to see the wisp being raised, so that it can tense its muscles in preparation as the wisp is "banged" down. The muscle area is then relaxed by a stroke with the stable rubber. These two actions are repeated in a steady rhythm, causing the horse alternately to tense and relax the muscles, which helps to tone them up. The wisp should not be used violently. The "bang" should be firm enough to cause the horse to tense but not so hard that it causes pain or fear. Take care to avoid bony areas like the shoulder blade or you will bruise and damage the underlying structures.

j. Grooming mitt – For removing grease and dust from the horse's

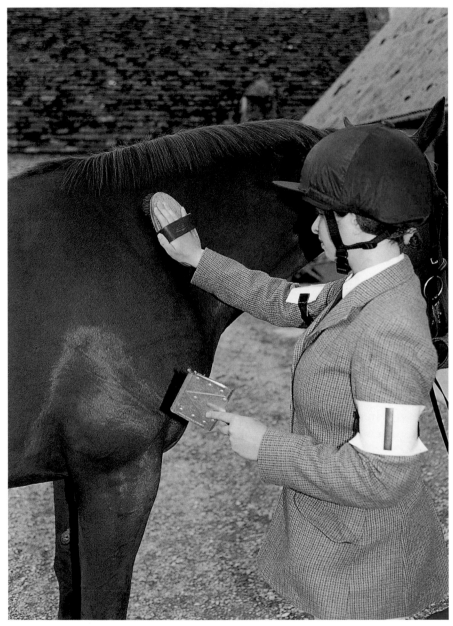

Grooming the horse with body brush and curry comb

This photograph was taken under examination conditions at The Talland School of Equitation

coat. It can be used on any part of the horse's body, including the head. A mitt is generally made of cactus cloth or rubber. Both types are stroked firmly over the body or used in a circular or to and fro action to remove dried sweat, mud, etc. The rubber type will lift grease to the surface, while the cactus cloth type will lift off surface grease/dust and help to create a shine on the coat.

k. Cactus cloth – Has the same use as the grooming mitt described above, but is in the form of a duster-sized cloth.

l. Water brush – For applying water to the coat/mane/tail in order to lay the hair or to wash it. It can be used on any part of the horse, including the feet.

m. Sponges – For washing the horse's eyes, nostrils and under the dock. You should have three separate sponges, one for each area, in different colours to avoid confusion.

3. Some General Points

a. Always tie your horse up before grooming it. You risk being cornered in the stable and may be kicked or bitten, especially if you are grooming a sensitive spot.

b. Remove water buckets before you begin grooming. The dust created during the grooming process will quickly make the water dirty. If the stable has an automatic water drinker, clean out the bowl when you have finished grooming.

c. All brushes can be used in a to and fro action, against the lie of the hair, to help to remove mud, grease, etc. However, you should always finish with a stroke that lays the hair flat in its direction of growth.

d. Brushes will not remove grease and mud from a wet coat, so leave a wet horse to dry before grooming.

e. When grooming the head, first untie the horse. Stand facing the horse. With one hand holding the head collar, use the other hand to body brush the front of the face. Start in the middle of the forehead and work upwards and outwards, and then down to the end of the nose. Then slip the head collar back around the horse's neck. To groom the nearside of the face, stand with your right shoulder under the horse's throat, put your right arm around the offside of its face and place your hand on its nose. Your left hand

*Grooming
the tail*

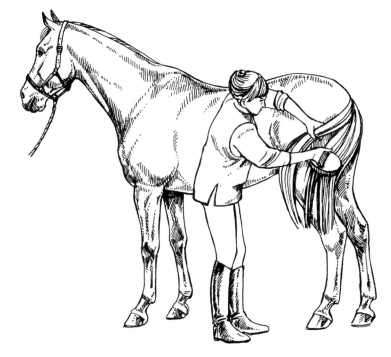

*Sponging
the eyes
and
nostrils*

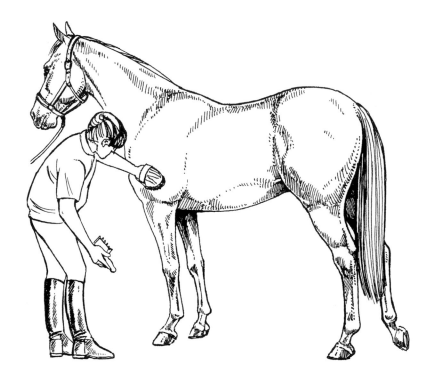

*Groom all
over the body
and legs*

is then free to brush the face. Repeat on the other side. Then
replace the head collar and tie up.

f. The head collar should never be put around the horse's neck
while the rope is tied to the wall. If the horse steps back or is star-
tled, the head collar may tighten around its throat or slip over its
head, causing the horse to panic and maybe break loose. Untie
the rope first and either place it over the horse's neck or leave it
loose in the string loop.

g. To groom the mane, brush all of it over on to the opposite side to
that on which it normally lies. With the body brush or mane
comb, bring a few hairs at a time towards you and brush thoroughly to remove dirt and tangles. Start at the poll and work
towards the withers until you have groomed the whole mane.

h. To groom the tail, stand to one side of the horse, never directly
behind it. Stand close in to the horse's quarters and take the
whole tail in one hand. With the other hand, use the body brush

to brush down a few hairs at a time. Difficult tangles
can be loosened with your fingers. You can
work through the whole tail with your
fingers if you prefer.

i. If your horse is quite tall,
stand on a stool or box to
make sure you get all of it
really clean.

j. While grooming, constantly
run your spare hand over the
horse. In this way you will feel
dirt, scabs, lumps, heat, etc., that
may be forming, for example under
the hair or under the belly and
which are not visible. This is especially important when grooming the legs. You should constantly compare the two forelegs and
the two hind legs, as this will help you to detect abnormalities at
the earliest possible stage.

k. Use your grooming time to learn about every inch of your horse.

l. Always put loose hair, and pick out feet, into a skip to keep the
yard area tidy.

m. Wash the whole grooming kit regularly. If you are using it every
day, it will probably need to be washed once a week. Wash it in
warm, soapy water. Washing-up liquid will do the job. Be careful
not to leave wooden or leather-backed brushes soaking as these
materials will soon rot or crack. Wash and rinse the brushes clean
of soap then leave them to drain and dry in a warm atmosphere.

- Brushes will not remove grease and mud from a wet coat, so leave a wet horse to dry before grooming

4. Method

Strapping

Strapping is the full grooming process, including wisping. Generally used
for the fit, stable-kept horse, strapping will take between 30–45 minutes to
complete.

a. Use a hoof pick to pick out the feet. Check the condition of the
feet and shoes at the same time.

b. Remove mud from the coat with the dandy brush.
c. Groom the mane and forelock with the body brush and/or mane comb.
d. Groom the head with the body brush.
e. Work over the whole body to bring all the grease to the surface with the rubber curry comb and/or the rubber grooming mitt.
f. Use the body brush and metal curry comb together to remove all the grease and dust.
g. Groom the tail with the body brush and your fingers.
h. Wisp if required.
i. Wash the eyes and nostrils and under the dock, with separate sponges and warm water.
j. Lay the mane and tail with the water brush.

Using the sweat scraper   **This photograph was taken under examination conditions at The Talland School of Equitation**

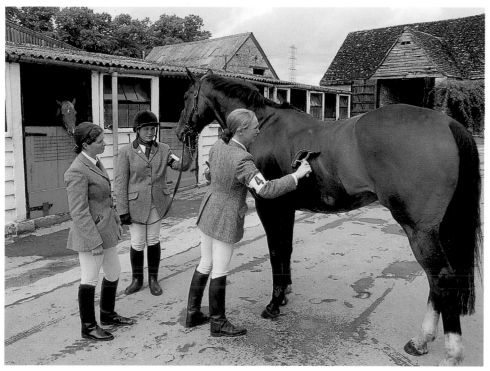

k. Put a final shine on the coat by dusting over with the stable rubber and / or the cactus cloth / mitt.

Grooming

Grooming is the basic cleaning of the horse. Generally used to prepare the field-kept horse / pony for work, grooming will take some 15–30 minutes to complete. "Grooming" is the word most commonly used to describe any brushing / cleaning of the horse.

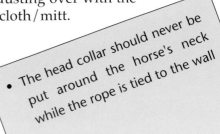

• The head collar should never be put around the horse's neck while the rope is tied to the wall

a. Pick out feet.
b. Remove mud and loose coat with the dandy brush and plastic curry comb.
c. Groom the mane and forelock with the body brush and / or mane comb.
d. Groom the head with the body brush.
e. Groom the tail with the body brush and your fingers.
f. In the summer, remove excess grease and dust by lightly body brushing all over. Do not remove too much grease as grease is essential for waterproofing and protection, especially in the winter.
g. Finally, wash the eyes, nostrils and under the dock.

Quartering

Quartering is the basic cleaning of the rugged, stable-kept horse prior to work, by folding back the rug in four successive quarters. Designed as a quick tidy-up session before riding, quartering should take only 10–15 minutes.

a. Pick out feet.
b. Remove stable stains from the legs with the dandy or body brush.
c. Groom the head with the body brush.
d. Tidy up the mane and tail and remove any bedding with the body brush.
e. Undo the breast and belly straps of the rug. Folding back a quar-

ter of the rug at a time, remove stable stains, etc., with the body brush.

f.   Use the water brush and warm water for any heavy stains that will not brush out.

g.   Finally, sponge the eyes, nostrils and under the dock.

5. The Grooming Machine

Although not found in every yard, the grooming machine is an excellent labour-saving device. There are many types: for example, hand-held or strapped to the waist. As with any electrical equipment, safety is very important. First check that the plug and lead are secure and that no wires are exposed. Once plugged in, make sure the lead cannot be trodden on by the horse. Suspend it from a hook or over a door. Some horses may be worried about the machine at first. However, if you introduce it carefully, most horses will soon settle. It may also help to accustom some horses to clipping machines if they have not been clipped before. A grooming machine works like a small vacuum cleaner, drawing the dust and grease out of the horse's coat and cleaning very thoroughly with little effort required from the groom. It is sometimes thought, however, that the horse misses out on the massaging effect created by manual grooming. If you have a grooming machine, it is a good idea to use it once or twice a week on each stabled horse and groom them manually on the other occasions.

Follow-up Work to Confirm Knowledge and Experience

1.   Working in a yard where there are both stable- and field-kept horses that need strapping/grooming/quartering every day is the best way to become practised and efficient at the job.

2.   Many new designs and items of grooming kit are constantly coming on to the market. Visit a local saddlery shop where you can look at, and familiarise yourself with, any new designs.

Helpful Hints and Exam Technique

 Remember that your hands are your best grooming tool. Make sure you do not wear gloves when grooming because you need to be able to feel for lumps, bumps, heat, etc.

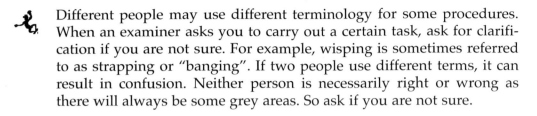 Different people may use different terminology for some procedures. When an examiner asks you to carry out a certain task, ask for clarification if you are not sure. For example, wisping is sometimes referred to as strapping or "banging". If two people use different terms, it can result in confusion. Neither person is necessarily right or wrong as there will always be some grey areas. So ask if you are not sure.

Always groom with vigour, even if you are just briefly demonstrating the use of a certain brush.

If you need to go in and out of the stable for equipment, always close and bolt the door behind you even if the horse is tied up.

It is easy to forget safe procedures when handling a quiet horse, especially if you know the horse quite well. In the exam, treat each horse as if you have never met it before. Don't walk or stand directly behind the horse. Don't make sudden or careless movements. Keep safety uppermost in your thoughts. Remember to replace the water buckets when you have finished and before you untie the horse.

2   Psychology and Behavioural Problems

By learning about the natural instincts of the horse and how domesticated horses of different types and ages may behave in various situations, and also why they do so, we can begin to understand equine behaviour. This, in turn, will aid safe and effective working practices with the horse as well as helping the individual to cope with horses which have developed behavioural problems. It will also encourage us to create a happy environment for the horse, which will help to minimise the likelihood of horses developing behavioural problems in the first place.

1.   Natural Instincts and Lifestyle

a.   The basic instincts to survive and reproduce govern the behaviour of the horse. The strongest, most dominant stallion will gather a group of mares and endeavour to protect them. There will also be a dominant mare who will lead the group.

b.   Horses are sociable animals, living together as a herd. Led by the dominant mare and stallion, stronger or weaker herd members will establish their place, resulting in an order similar to the "pecking order" among chickens. Many smaller groups of friends will also form within the herd.

c.   Horses are not predatory animals, but would have been preyed upon in the wild. They instinctively flee from danger, using their speed to escape from their attacker. It is important that the whole herd should keep together if danger threatens as groups are less vulnerable to attack than individuals. Therefore, if one horse takes flight, the whole herd will respond and go too.

d.   The horse's sense of hearing is very acute. Their mobile ears constantly move to listen for danger that may approach from any direction. Likewise, their eyes are set on the sides of their faces

13

Horses relaxed and grazing in the field

for good peripheral vision. They have a small blind spot immediately behind and in front of them but can move their heads
around in order to see if predators are approaching. The horse's
head and ear movements are a constant indication of what it is
thinking and feeling.

e. If cornered and unable to take flight, the horse will try to defend
itself. It can turn its hind legs towards the attacker and lash out
or can bite and strike out with a foreleg.

f. Horses graze throughout the day, keeping the stomach supplied
with food but never letting it become full. This enables them to
take flight at any time without having the restriction of a full
stomach pressing against their lungs.

g. Horses rest by sleeping on their feet. Again, they can quickly take flight from this position. However, if the weather is fine and the sun shining, they like to lie down providing there is no imminent threat of danger. One or more members of the group will remain standing, as "lookouts" for the herd.

h. All horses enjoy rolling. It helps to remove old winter coat and camouflages the horse by covering it in mud.

i. A horse can scratch many parts of its body with its teeth. However, as it cannot reach its own withers, it will approach and scratch the withers of another horse. This will stimulate the other horse into reciprocal scratching.

j. Colts and fillies will be boisterous together. Through play, they learn about adult behaviour and mutual respect.

k. Older horses will tolerate playful youngsters unless they become particularly boisterous. They may then bite or kick to establish their superiority and put the youngster in its place.

2. The Domesticated Horse in the Field

In many ways field-kept horses have a fairly natural lifestyle.

a. They will take flight as a herd if danger threatens.

b. They will take turns lying down and keeping watch.

c. They will form smaller groups of friends within a large group.

d. They will establish who is the strongest and therefore the leader.

e. When relaxed, they will be seen grazing, spread out across the field, standing nose to tail swishing flies from each other's faces or scratching each other's withers.

f. If one horse is standing alone and obviously separate from the herd, not appearing to join in with the others, you should suspect something is wrong and investigate the situation. Likewise, if all the horses suddenly took flight across the field and began galloping around, you should look for the cause.

g. Mares and geldings should be separated in the spring and summer. This helps to prevent injuries occurring when geldings begin to behave like stallions by singling out mares in season and also fighting with each other.

All horses enjoy rolling

Mutual scratching has benefit for both participants

Young horses like to play

h. After its companions have been taken away, a horse left on its own in the field may panic. It will call, trot up and down the fence and possibly try to jump out as instinct tells it to follow the herd. The same situation is likely to occur if two particular friends are separated, despite there being other companions available. However, horses soon adjust to being taken in and out of the field, providing more than one is left behind for company.

i. One young and one old horse kept together may not enjoy each other's company. The young one will want to play, which may bother the older horse. However, several youngsters kept together will play happily, while older horses graze and rest quietly.

j. In wet and windy weather, or when hot and bothered by flies, the horses will group together in sheltered areas. A horse alone in these conditions will either be wet and miserable with cold, without its companions to help to shelter it, or will run around the field in distress trying to escape flies that it cannot defeat on its own.

k. In the confines of the field, a stronger horse may corner a weaker member of the group and defensive behaviour will be seen. The horses will kick out at each other or use their teeth to bite. Those with a more timid nature may try to jump out of the field rather than defend themselves.

l. If a new horse is introduced to an established group, there will be a period of adjustment. This horse will have to establish its place in the herd. If it is quite dominant in nature, there may be a lot of fighting if it challenges the leaders of the herd. If it is more timid in nature, it will probably settle quite quickly, not posing a threat to any of the others. Initially, the rest of the herd will gather together and approach the new arrival. They will smell each other and there is likely to be kicking, squealing and some cantering around. The new arrival will also spend some time exploring its new surroundings. It will take at least a day to settle in.

m. If a horse has, for some reason, been stabled for a long period, it will take great delight in being returned to the more natural environment of the field. Typical behaviour includes galloping, rolling, exploring the field, smelling droppings left by other horses, bucking, snorting and, with all the senses alert, surveying its new surroundings.

3. Horses that are Difficult to Catch

Some horses become difficult to catch as soon as the spring grass comes through. Others develop a mistrust of people and learn that they can avoid being caught and thereby escape ill treatment. Some stabled horses, which are only turned out occasionally, can be difficult to catch when they are given their freedom. There are many different ways of catching these horses. The method employed depends on the horse and the situation.

a. The horse's attitude, particularly its ears, will give an indication of how easy or difficult it may be to catch. Ears back and swinging its head towards you in a threatening attitude is an obvious indication of its unwillingness. The same attitude is seen when one horse warns another not to come near feed, for example.

b. The horse may simply walk away or, if being more threatening, turn its quarters towards you, ready to kick.

c. The natural instinct to follow the herd can be helpful. If all the other horses in the field can be caught and brought into the yard, the last horse often allows itself to be caught in order to go with the herd.

d. In the same way, a loose horse may follow its friends in from the field and allow you to catch it when it reaches the stables. This only works if the track from field to yard is secure and not open to the road, for example.

e. A bucket of feed can be a good tempter, providing there are no other horses in the field.

f. If you leave a head collar on in the field, make sure it is a leather one which will break if the horse gets caught up. Attach a short piece of string, approximately 30 cm (1 ft) long, to help you to take hold of the horse when you go to catch it.

g. Some horses will give in if you are persistent and follow them around for long enough.

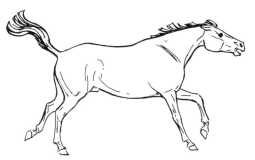

The horse may display aggressive behaviour as demonstrated in these two examples: (left) charging, with mouth open and ready to bite and (below) ears back, tail raised, and head thrust forward

h. For horses which are particularly difficult, a very small turn out paddock can be a good compromise.

i. Try to prevent this annoying vice by making sure that your horse enjoys itself when caught; for example, give a feed and don't always work the horse. Also, make sure that stabled horses are turned out frequently.

4. The Stabled Horse

This is the most unnatural way of life for a horse. As a result, problems and vices often develop.

a. If stabled, the horse should be provided with an environment in which it feels safe and where it can be provided with its daily needs.

b. A horse that is happy in its stable will appear relaxed, eat well, greet its owner at the door, lie down, or doze while standing, and generally display normal behaviour.

c. Confined to a stable, the horse cannot take flight if threatened. Its only option is to defend itself by biting or kicking. To prevent this dangerous behaviour, it is very important to handle the horse in a quiet, kind and confident manner, making it feel safe and relaxed in its stable.

d. Signs of unhappiness or distress will include threatening the owner with ears back and teeth showing; swinging hindquarters towards the door; not eating; box walking and weaving; rushing to and fro in the box, pushing at the door and calling; passing loose droppings; jumping back and snorting at any movements or noise.

e. Being separated from the herd can lead to stable vices like weaving and box walking, but careful planning can help to make the horse feel more relaxed. For example, American barn stabling allows the horses to see and smell each other so that they continue to feel like part of a herd.

f. Very young horses will not take kindly to being kept in individual boxes where their freedom and social activity are restricted. Keeping them together in barns can solve many problems. This system can help to preserve your grazing during wet, winter weather, while providing the youngsters with dry, sheltered conditions.

g. When we restrict its intake of feed, the horse's need to be almost constantly grazing may lead to vices like crib biting and wind sucking. By feeding little and often, with as constant a supply of hay/carrots/swede as possible for the horse to nibble, we can minimise these problems.

- If a new horse is introduced to an established group, there will be a period of adjustment

h. The horse's acute hearing will pick up anything happening around the yard. However, when confined to the stable it may not be able to see what is causing the noise. This may lead to the horse fretting and becoming nervous. For this reason, keep noise and disturbance to a minimum.

i. Consider the horse's temperament when deciding where to stable it. A stallion will want to see all activity as horses leave and enter the yard so that he feels he is watching over his herd. A timid horse may be miserable stabled between two very dominant horses. Horses lacking confidence will fret if stabled where they can constantly see other horses leaving the yard, as this will make them feel that the herd is leaving without them.

j. Horses of a nervous disposition will benefit from being stabled where they can see several other horses and communicate with them. This should also help you to gain their confidence as they will be able to see that the other horses trust you.

k. When approaching a nervous horse in its box, encourage it to come to the door to greet you first. Perhaps offer a handful of grass (or carrot, etc.), to bring the horse to the door. Allow the horse to smell and identify you, then slip in and put on a head collar.

- If stabled, the horse should be provided with an environment in which it feels safe and where it can be provided with its daily needs

l. Don't attempt to go in and

handle the horse without putting on a head collar. This could lead to the horse cornering you and you resorting to aggressive behaviour in order to escape. This will not be conducive to gaining the horse's confidence.

m. The aim is to handle the horse calmly and gently. Make your movements slow and gain the horse's confidence through handling it frequently, giving it time to get to know you and your yard routine.

n. "Routine" includes how you carry out tasks, not just the time at which you do them. This is particularly important when trying to gain the confidence of a nervous horse, or when teaching good behaviour to a young horse. For example, if you tie the horse up outside its stable to tack it up, keep to this routine. Don't suddenly change to tacking up inside the stable, or vice versa.

o. One of the most important points of good horsemastership is to treat each horse as an individual. Different characteristics and behavioural problems require different approaches.

5. The Horse when Ridden

Many different factors will affect the horse's behaviour when ridden, for example the mood and character of both horse and rider, as well as the situation and task to be tackled. Remember that, when handling horses, we take the place of the leader of the herd. If the horse is confident in us as its leader, it will do as we ask. When it loses confidence in us, problems begin.

Riding Out/Hacking

a. While all horses will spook at times, some horses seem to be far spookier than others. This may be due to a lack of confidence in their rider or they may just be a naturally timid horse.

b. If the rider is nervous, the horse will feel this and become nervous itself, its instinct telling it that if the rider is worried then there must be danger around the corner.

c. When being ridden through the countryside, your horse will be on a constant lookout for danger. Bushes, hedges and banks could all be places where a predator may be hiding, therefore it may be reluctant to approach or may try to give such things a wide berth. A confident rider will reassure the horse by riding forward calmly but firmly. Hitting or shouting at the horse will only worry it and make the problem worse.

d. A nervous horse is likely to become nappy, spooky, buck, jog, etc. Again, the horse's ears will be the rider's main indicator of what it might be thinking.

e. Many horses learn that, with some riders, when they spook they temporarily unbalance their riders and escape from being between leg and hand.

f. If the rider is not quick to regain command of the situation, the horse will take charge.

g. If the rider is confident and clear in his or her commands, the horse will settle and gradually gain confidence.

h. The herd instinct will lead to problems if you try to separate horses while out on a hack. Likewise, if one horse shies at an object, all the other horses will shy too.

i. A young horse will be in particular need of a confident rider as it will be experiencing many strange sights and sounds for the first time.

j. A nappy horse is one which tries to go against its rider's wishes by refusing to go in a particular direction, down a particular path or over a particular obstacle. As the argument goes on, it will also buck and/or rear as well as run backwards or try to rush off in a different direction.

k. Many ponies nap to a lesser degree by dragging their young rider back to their stable or back to the gate, despite the young rider's attempts to stop them.

l. Napping generally starts when the horse or pony realises that the rider is not in control. Some horses take charge and refuse to move or take the rider to the nearest feed bucket. In this situation, the horse is not frightened, just a dominant character with a weak rider.

m. If the horse realises that the rider is not in control and becomes frightened by the situation, then the nappy reaction is likely to be more extreme. If a confident rider takes over, the horse will continue to nap until the new rider has rebuilt the horse's confidence.

n. The longer the horse has been getting away with being nappy, the longer it will take to put the problem right. In fact, it may never be possible to eradicate the problem completely.

o. Another cause of nappiness is discomfort. This can arise if the horse's tack doesn't fit, if it has a problem with its teeth, a girth gall is forming, or there is any other problem that causes pain and therefore fear. In such circumstances, the horse is likely to nap in its attempts to get away from the problem causing the discomfort. It is therefore advisable to try to eliminate any such possible causes before taking firmer action with the horse.

p. In some situations, nappiness may be due to overfeeding. If the horse is having little exercise and large amounts of concentrate feed, it may be so full of energy that it doesn't know what to do with itself. Consequently, it begins behaving badly. The first indication for the rider is when he or she gets on the horse. If the horse is feeling tense, it may lift its back and feel as if it is about to buck. A swishing tail will also indicate tension.

q. Excess energy is often a reason for bucking. A horse full of fun and energy may buck to help itself let off steam, not just physically but also mentally.

r. Likewise, jogging can be a result of mental tension. For example, a highly-strung Thoroughbred, which has been hunting, may begin jogging when taken out on a hack, due to anticipating what it will be asked to do.

s. Jogging can also result from discomfort. The horse's instinct to take flight from danger leads it into trying to get away from whatever is hurting it. Pulling and snatching at the reins often accompanies the problem of jogging as the rider tries to restrain the horse and the horse tries to escape.

t. An unbalanced and not very good rider will cause the horse discomfort and this can lead to jogging, bucking or napping.

u. In all these situations, the rider must first look carefully for the cause of the problem. It may be necessary to enlist the help of a second opinion from someone who can look at the problem objectively. Remove the cause then rebuild the horse's confidence.

v. Relieve tension in the horse by being careful not to overfeed and, once again, take care with your stable management. For example, turn out regularly, stable in a calm atmosphere with companion-ship and follow a regular exercise routine.

Follow-up Work to Confirm Knowledge and Experience

1. Keeping the horse's natural instincts uppermost in your mind, observe horses in as many different situations as possible – in the stable yard, in the field, at shows, at stud farms, at sales – and keep asking yourself why those particular horses are behaving in that particular way.
2. When working with your own horses, if you come across any problems, try to analyse how you could improve the horse's environment with due regard for natural instincts and see if you can successfully solve the problem.

Helpful Hints and Exam Technique

When answering questions in a theoretical situation, try to picture horses with which you have had experience. Whenever possible, answer the questions by using real examples. In this way your answers are more likely to have an authentic ring to them, showing the examiner that you really are experienced and have a good understanding of the subject.

Try not to disagree with other candidates' answers. If someone makes a statement with which you disagree, state your own opinion but remember that they may have experienced different situations to you and it may be that you are both correct. There are many situations in which there is no one correct answer, where everyone's comments can be valid.

3   The Field-kept Horse and Grassland Management

The needs of the horse at grass are many and varied. Through good management and regular maintenance, we can provide a horse with a suitable environment and good grazing.

1. Fencing

General Points

a. The type of fencing you do choose will depend upon financial constraints, type of horse and existing fencing, hedges, etc.
b. Three rails or strands of wire will discourage horses from reaching through the fence. This reduces the likelihood of broken fences and escape.
c. The bottom rail/wire should be approximately 45 cm (18 in) from the ground. This allows horses to graze immediately under the fence but is too low for them to roll underneath it. If it is any lower than this, horses may get a foot caught over the bottom rail/wire.
d. The top rail/wire should be approximately 135 cm (53 in) high.
e. Posts are placed 5–6 m (16–19 ft) apart.
f. For Shetland ponies, you will need to lower these measurements, or use a different type of fencing, as Shetlands would escape easily under the bottom wire.
g. As horses are inclined to lean against fencing, wire and rails should be fixed to the inside of the posts, to prevent them from springing off.

Types of Fencing

a. Post and rail – Usually constructed of wood, although other

Some of the problems caused by using unsuitable fencing

materials, such as metal rails and concrete posts, can be used.
Although expensive, post and rail provides a strong visible
fence. The wood should be treated with a weatherproof preserv-
ative and will last longer if repainted each year. If the wood is not
properly cared for and maintained it will rot, break and splinter,
rendering it more easily broken by the inhabitants of the field,
which could prove very hazardous.

b. Post and wire – Less expensive and therefore frequently used.
Plain wire is best for horses, although it will stretch when leant
on, therefore it should be frequently checked and made taut.
Barbed wire may command more respect but poses a problem as
it can cause horrific injuries. New Zealand rugs are frequently
torn on barbed wire. Rail and wire are often combined with a top

Good secure fencing. Rails should be fixed to the inside of the fence posts, to prevent them from springing off if horses push against them

rail and two lower strands of wire, or a top and bottom rail with a strand of wire between.

c. Hedges – Providing they are not poisonous and are checked for poisonous plants, hedges make good natural barriers which prevent horses from leaning against or reaching through the wire/rail with which they can be combined.

d. Electric – Initially, electric fencing was unsuitable for horses as it was thin wire that they tended to run through and so become entangled. Now, reels of plastic fencing with thin strands of wire running through it are available. This fencing comes in broad strips and various colours, making it highly visible. It has insulators and joining buckles which make it possible to erect the fencing just like post and rail. It has the advantage that horses will not lean on it.

e. Stud/stock fencing – This comes in various forms, the aim being to provide safe fencing for small, valuable foals, boisterous youngsters or any other horse for that matter. A wire mesh is used, with a close enough weave to prevent small feet from becoming trapped. This may be topped with a strip of rubber fencing which adds visibility and will not cause damage if run into.

f. Gates – As an essential part of the fencing, gates should open into the field, which helps to prevent horses from barging out, and should be wide enough for farm machinery to gain access. To deter thieves, the top hinge pin should be turned over to prevent the gate from being lifted off its hinges and the gate should be padlocked at both ends. Choose a latch that locks in place and cannot be opened by the horse.

2. Water

A constant fresh supply must be provided.

a. Natural sources – A running stream that comes from an unpolluted source is suitable, providing there is firm standing where the horses can approach. Any natural source that becomes stagnant, comes from a polluted area or has a very muddy approach should be fenced off and not used.

b. Self-filling trough – The most convenient way of supplying water to the field. The trough should be positioned away from trees, to prevent leaves and debris falling in, and away from the gate, to prevent crowding in this area, but close enough for easy checking. It should also be well away from the fence, to allow the horses to visit the trough without getting trapped, or form part of the fence in order to supply two fields at once.

c. Other systems – Various different troughs and buckets can be used and filled manually. The important points to remember are:

the trough/bucket must be stable and not easily knocked over; there should be no sharp edges, handles or protrusions that a horse could be injured on; it must be cleaned and topped up frequently.

- Gates are an essential part of the fencing. They should open into the field, which helps to prevent horses from barging out if they lean on the gate or if one horse is lead out of the field, leaving others behind

3. Shelter

Horses need protection from the wind and rain in the winter and should be provided with shade in the summer.

- a. Natural – Trees and hedges provide the best form of shelter for large groups of horses. They can then group themselves, without fighting, in the most sheltered or shaded part of the field.
- b. Erected constructions – Suitable for smaller groups they should be positioned to protect horses from the prevailing wind. A three-sided construction allows for easy access, and also escape, through the open side. The shelter should be large enough to accommodate all the horses.

4. Poisonous Plants and Trees

It is important to recognise poisonous plants, not to just know their names. Knowing where they are likely to grow is also helpful.

Poisonous trees and hedges should be fenced off and kept well cut back to prevent horses reaching them over the fence. Oak trees pose a particular problem as they drop acorns each autumn. Acorns are relished by many horses and can lead to severe cases of colic. The best policy is to avoid such fields in the autumn. Squirrels will help to clear the acorns which can also be rolled. This partly crushes them and squashes them into the ground.

Poisonous plants should be pulled up before they go to seed, where possible, to prevent them from spreading. Some, like buttercups, may only be eradicated with the use of weed killers.

Ragwort, the best known of plants poisonous to horses, is rarely eaten

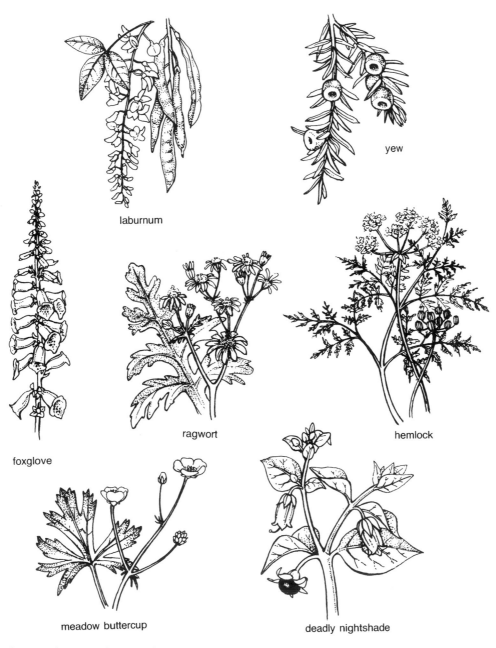

laburnum

yew

foxglove

ragwort

hemlock

meadow buttercup

deadly nightshade

Some poisonous plants and trees

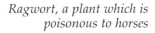

Ragwort, a plant which is poisonous to horses

when growing providing the horse has sufficient grazing. However, when wilted or dried, it becomes more palatable although it is still poisonous. It is advisable to burn the plants after pulling them up. Hay should not be made from fields containing ragwort.

Ornamental plants, trees and shrubs are likely to be poisonous. If in doubt, fence them off or remove them. Many of the poisons are accumulative. If your horse eats a plant with no apparent ill effects, it doesn't necessarily mean you should let it go on eating more.

The poisonous plants most commonly found are:

- *Plants*: foxgloves, bracken, hemlock, ivy, ragwort, buttercups, deadly and woody nightshade.
- *Trees*: yew, oak, laburnum.
- *Hedges*: privet, laurel, rhododendron.

5. Maintaining Good Pasture

a. Areas of grass that taste sweetest to the horse are grazed very short, like lawns. If the field is overgrazed, these "lawns" become patchy and grazing is ruined for the future. Fields should be rested as the grass gets short, to allow for a period of regrowth. How often, and how long, the field is rested depends upon the number of horses grazing and the speed of regrowth. In spring, given warm weather and rain, the grass will grow rapidly.

b. Horses avoid grazing soured areas of grass where they have left their droppings. This creates a wasted area of long, rough grass. These "roughs" should be topped. This means that they are cut short in order to encourage dense growth, rather than sparse areas of long grass that the horses will continue to avoid grazing. If available, sheep and cattle will top the long grass, being less fussy eaters than horses.

c. As well as making the grazing unpalatable to the horse, droppings contain worm larvae which will spread on to the grass, be eaten by the grazing horses and thus increase each horse's worm burden. If the paddock is small, the droppings should be removed daily. As this is not practical in large fields, they should be spread out with a harrow. Once spread, earthworms, rain, dung beetles, etc., will quickly work the droppings into the soil. At the same time, the larvae will be exposed to the weather and some may be destroyed before they can be eaten. A practical alternative to harrowing is now available in the form of a large vacuum machine mounted on the back of a Land-Rover or tractor, which vacuums up the droppings.

Using a vacuum machine, attached to a vehicle, to remove droppings. An alternative to harrowing

d. Apart from removing droppings, the worm burden on the field can be reduced by periodically grazing sheep and cattle. They eat the horse worm larvae which are unable to survive in other animals, thus breaking the cycle and reducing the worm burden.

e. Plants like nettles and thistles will also need to be removed from the field. Although they are not poisonous, they will compete with the grass, leaving your field with more weed than grazing.

- Learn to identify a variety of the most common plants found and keep in practice. It is important to recognise poisonous plants, not just to know their names

Again, regular topping and/or grazing sheep and cattle will help to keep these plants, and others like them, under control. Many horses enjoy eating wilted thistles and nettles, so they can be left in the field when cut.

f. Seek advice about fertiliser from an expert, as this may be needed and should be applied in spring or autumn.

If you don't follow these procedures, you will end up with a horse-sick paddock. This is a paddock with obvious lawns and roughs, an excess amount of droppings, bare and poached areas and weeds and poisonous plants in abundance, and it will carry a very heavy worm burden.

6. Daily Checks

The field-kept horse and its field must be checked several times every day. It only takes a few moments for a piece of fencing to be broken or for one horse to kick and injure another. Either of these incidents could have dire results if left unchecked for any length of time. Early-morning and late-evening checks are essential as the horse will have been, or will be about to be, left unseen through the night period. Throughout the day, look in on the horse as frequently as possible.

a. Check that the horse is behaving normally, shows no signs of ill health and has not sustained any injuries. Pick out its feet and check the shoes.

b. If the horse is rugged, check that the fastenings are secure, replace the rug if it has slipped, look for tears and check that the rug is dry inside.

c. Look at the fencing and gate. Are they secure?

d. Is the water supply flowing and clean?

e. Look for poisonous plants and weeds, especially in the spring.

f. Make sure no debris has found its way into the field. There may be a tin can, plastic bag, etc., that needs removing.

g. Shelters should be checked in case of broken boards or maybe a hole in the roof.

Follow-up Work to Confirm Knowledge and Experience

1. Observe various types of fencing, watering systems, shelter, etc., and see which you think work best and why.

Helpful Hints and Exam Technique

 At Stage Two you need to be able to describe various poisonous plants. Make sure you really know what they look like, what colour of flowers they have, how tall they grow and where you are most likely to find them growing.

4   Feeding

In order to be able to feed suitable types and quantities of feed to a variety of different horses and ponies, it is necessary to recognise different feedstuffs, good and bad quality and understand the horse's nutritional needs.

1. The Rules of Feeding and Watering

a. Feed little and often – This method closely resembles horses' natural way of feeding. When not stabled, they graze and keep their relatively small stomachs constantly about half-full.

b. Only feed good quality feedstuffs – Poor quality feeds can contain mould spores which lead to respiratory disorders and are low in nutritional value, leading to unthriftiness in the horse.

c. Feed at regular intervals daily – Within the daily routine, horses soon learn to expect their feeds at certain times. Delay in feeding can lead to frustration and problems such as door banging. At competitions, normal feeding times may need to be adjusted. However, the change in routine, new surroundings, etc., should keep the horse occupied so it may not be so aware of the change in feeding times.

d. Use only clean receptacles to hold feed and water – Old food or debris of any sort left in the feed or water bowl will smell unpalatable and discourage the horse from eating the fresh food or drinking the water.

e. A supply of fresh water must be constantly available – Water is essential for all body functions. Approximately 70 per cent of the adult horse's bodyweight is water.

f. Do not feed directly before exercise – The stomach lies behind the diaphragm. When full, it will press against the diaphragm, restricting expansion of the lungs. At the same time, digestion will slow down as exercise starts. Allow a minimum of one hour after feeding before exercising.

g. Remove water approximately one hour before strenuous exercise – This is only necessary if your horse is likely to drink large amounts prior to fast work such as racing or advanced eventing. For the same reasons as above, too much water in the stomach will restrict expansion of the lungs.

h. Water before feeding – Although water should be constantly available, the horse will be deprived of it at times, for example during exercise. Therefore, on return, offer water before feed or the horse may be tempted to eat first, then drink a large quantity of water. This may cause the feed to swell rapidly, as well as diluting the digestive juices and washing feed rapidly through the system, leading to colic or poor digestion.

i. Change water buckets a minimum of three times daily – Water left standing in the stable will absorb ammonia. It should be tipped away and replaced with fresh water.

j. Do not make any sudden changes to the horse's diet – The horse has bacteria in its large intestine, which help it to digest specific feeds. If new feeds are intro-duced gradually, the bacteria have time to adjust. Sudden changes will upset the bacterial bal-ance, leading to poorly digested feed and colic.

k. Feed something succulent daily – Succulent feeds are enjoyed by the horse. When mixed with dry feeds, they improve mastication and diges-tion.

- The amount of feed to give the horse each day is arrived at by calculating 2.5 per cent of the horse's body weight, and then feeding approximately 4–5 lb (1.8–2.2 kg) less of that figure

l. Feed plenty of bulk – As the horse's system is designed to digest large amounts, plenty of bulk and roughage are needed to aid digestion of all feeds and keep the system in good working order.

m. Give water in small amounts on return from strenuous exercise – After an event or race, when the horse is hot and breathing heav-ily, water intake should be restricted. Offer 2–3 litres (4–6 pt) at a time, every five minutes (take the chill off by adding some warm water to the bucket), until the horse has quenched its thirst. It can then be left with a normal water supply. This process prevents large amounts of cold water shocking the system while it is returning to normal.

n. Feed according to:

- work being done
- age
- time of year
- whether field-kept or stabled
- height and build
- ability of rider
- temperament

All these factors influence the type and quantity of feed. Harder work requires more energy-giving feed, while a laxative diet is needed if the horse is stabled and off work. Youngsters need body-building material; old horses may need softer, cooked foods that are easy to chew and digest. Field-kept horses need food for warmth in winter, while those that are stabled can wear extra rugs. Larger horses need more feed than smaller ones but a large horse with a novice rider should not receive a high-energy diet which may make it difficult to manage. Whatever the size, age, etc., the temperament can vary. You should avoid giving oats to a more excitable type but may find that a more placid horse does very well on them.

2. Feeding and Watering Systems

Feeding Receptacles

a. Choose a feed bowl that will not constitute a hazard when empty. A horse left with an empty bucket with a handle can easily catch its leg in the handle and be injured.

b. Bowls that stand on the floor can be secured within a car tyre. Even if the horse pulls the empty bowl out of the tyre, there are no sharp edges that could cause damage.

c. Mangers that hook over the door work well for some horses. As the design with metal hooks is potentially dangerous, the plastic type is preferable.

Feed mangers suitable for stable use: the door manger (left) *is removed after feeding and* (right) *the corner manger is usually a permanent fixture*

    d. Mangers that slot into a wall fixing also work well. Check that the fixing has no sharp edges as many horses remove their mangers when they are empty.

    e. Use a manger or feed bowl that can be cleaned easily.

Feeding Hay to Stabled Horses

    a. Hay can be fed from the floor. However, it often gets mixed into the horse's bedding which is wasteful and can encourage the horse to eat its bed.

    b. Hay nets are useful, making the weighing of quantities easy, especially if a spring balance is used. When empty, however, hay

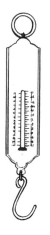

A spring balance for weighing hay in a hay net

nets are potentially dangerous as the horse can catch a foot in one and get stuck. They must be tied high off the floor, very securely, be checked frequently and removed as soon as they are empty.

c. Hay racks are another alternative. To prevent the horse from getting its legs caught, the rack must be fixed quite high. This is a drawback as it means the horse must stretch upwards to eat, allowing hay seeds to fall in its eyes and the underline muscles of the neck to become overdeveloped.

Feeding Hay to Field-kept Horses

a. Feeding directly from the ground is the best method. Put out several more piles of hay than the number of horses feeding. In this way, if one horse chases another away, there will always be a spare pile for that horse to move to. To help to prevent poaching, feed the hay in different areas of the field each day.

b. Hay racks are an alternative but are heavy to move around. Also, if one horse chases another away, that horse may end up with no feed at all.

c. Hay nets are dangerous in the field. It would be difficult to tie them high enough for safety and if one fell down or a horse got its leg caught, it could go unnoticed for some time.

Watering the Field-kept Horse

a. The most basic way of providing water in the field or stable is to use buckets that must be checked and refilled frequently. As mentioned above, however, buckets with handles can be a hazard if knocked over.

b. For several horses in one field, a plastic or metal trough, which can be filled using a hose, is an option. Daily checks will ensure that the trough is clean and full.

c. Self-filling troughs are labour saving but daily checks are just as essential to ensure that the trough is working correctly and is full and clean.

d. Troughs and buckets should be situated away from trees and hedges to prevent debris from falling in. They should not be so close to the gate that the entrance becomes blocked when horses gather for water but, if nearby, they will probably be checked more frequently. Troughs should be well clear of the fence to allow the horses free access all round and to prevent kicking and cornering. Alternatively, they can be sited to form part of the fence. This is helpful in adjoining fields, as one trough can supply both at once.

e. A stream may provide an adequate water supply but you need to be sure that it does not come from a polluted source. Sandy-bottomed streams may result in sand colic as horses are likely to swallow sand when drinking. An approach area of firm standing will be necessary.

f. Access to ponds and any areas of polluted or stagnant water should be fenced off.

g. Troughs and buckets must be checked several times a day in winter to make sure ice is broken.

Watering the Stabled Horse

a. Automatic water drinkers are useful. They provide a constant supply of water in small quantities, which saves wastage and is labour saving. However, it is not always possible to tell how much the horse is drinking. The water bowl must be cleaned out daily and checked frequently to make sure it is not full of hay or bedding. In winter, an alternative method of watering may be required if the system freezes.

b. Buckets, again without handles, work well. They should be secured in a car tyre for stability.

3. Types of Feed and their Preparation

Hay – Some General Points

a. The quality of hay depends on when it was cut, how quickly it was dried, whether the pasture was free from weeds and the types of grass it is made from.

b. If the hay is cut early, the grass will still be very leafy and moist. A lengthy drying process may cause the leaf to disintegrate and make the hay very dusty. Large amounts of clover in the hay lead to the same problem. If cut too late, the grasses will have gone to seed and lost much of their nutritional value. At the same time, through exposure to wet weather, moulds may have started to form.

c. If dried quickly, the hay will maintain its nutritional value and contain little dust. However, if it rains and the hay is left out for several days, mould spores will multiply and the hay will quickly deteriorate and be very dusty.

d. Weeds reduce the feed quality of the hay and can be dangerous. Ragwort, for example, will be readily eaten when dried but is still poisonous. If it goes unnoticed in the hay ration, it could prove fatal.

e. Good quality grasses give the hay a higher nutritional value.

f. If the hay is baled before it is sufficiently dry, it will heat up in the stack and moulds will form.

g. Visibly mouldy hay should not be fed to horses. The tiny mould spores will pass into the horse's lungs, causing inflammation and coughing.

h. The cleanest-looking hay can still carry mould spores. Soaking the hay in clean water will cause the mould spores to swell to a size that prevents them from being inhaled into the lungs, therefore it is advisable to feed soaked hay.

i. Good quality hay smells fresh, tastes sweet, looks clean and, when shaken out, doesn't appear to be dusty.

j. Poor quality hay will smell mouldy, look grey and dirty and be very dusty when shaken out. If you can see mouldy patches, it is very poor indeed.

k. Hay is a bulk feed. As the horse's digestive system is designed to digest large amounts of bulk, hay and its alternatives should form a large part of most horses' diets.

Meadow Hay

a. This is made from permanent pasture and contains a variety of grasses.

- Self-filling troughs are labour saving but daily checks are just as essential to ensure that the trough is working correctly and is full and clean

b. It is the type of hay most frequently fed to horses and is fairly soft and palatable.

Seed Hay

a. This is a crop grown from specially selected seeds. Rye grass is normally used.
b. It is quite a hard hay and more difficult to digest than meadow hay. However, providing it is well made, it has a higher nutritional value and is often used for competition horses.

Threshed Hay

a. This hay is grown from seed in order to produce more seeds that will be sold. It is cut and then threshed to remove the seeds.
b. Good quality grass will be used and, if well made, the hay can be of medium quality. The threshing process will have "battered" the grass and may make it more prone to being dusty.

Haylage

a. This is semi-wilted, vacuum-packed grass.
b. Once the air is excluded, a small amount of fermentation takes place but moulds do not form. This leaves us with a dust-free alternative to hay.
c. The nutritional value of haylage is higher than that of hay, so smaller quantities are usually fed.

Barley

a. Barley is usually fed rolled or crushed, to aid digestion.
b. It is also fed boiled. Put the whole grains in water then bring them to the boil and simmer until the grains have swollen and burst open. This makes a warm, tasty, tempting and easily digested feed for a tired horse, especially in winter.
c. There is also cooked, flaked barley, micronised barley and extruded barley. For each different type the manufacturer uses a different cooking process. These processes destroy some of the feed value of the barley but make it easier to digest.

Types of feed: (above) *seed hay, haylage, meadow hay and* (below) *whole barley*

Different feeds (starting at top left, reading clockwise): sugar beet cubes, horse and pony cubes, coarse mix, barley, oats, and soaked sugar beet

A good variety of feed is essential to ensure the good health and well-being of horses. Different feeds are illustrated in these two pages

Horse and pony nuts

Coarse mix

Rolled oats

Rolled barley

These two feeds are sugar beet, before and after soaking

Alfalfa

Bran

d. A good sample of barley should be similar to oats but there will be no separate outer husk.

e. Barley is mainly an energy-giving feed. It does not tend to make horses as excitable as oats do but it does have a tendency to make them fat.

Oats

a. Whole oats may pass through the horse's system undigested as they have a hard outer layer that the horse has difficulty in digesting. For this reason, oats are usually fed rolled, as with barley. This rolling process breaks open the oat to expose the nutritious part, the kernel. However, once rolled, the oats will begin to lose their feed value and should be fed within a couple of weeks of purchase.

b. Oats have a thin outer husk that breaks away from the grain. This husk adds fibre to the diet and encourages the horse to chew the oats thoroughly.

c. A good sample should have an equal mix of husk and grain, rather than large amounts of husk. It should be free from dust and any sign of mould. The grain should be clean and fawn-coloured, with a white kernel.

d. Oats are mainly an energy-giving feed and should only be fed to horses in hard work. Some horses become overly excitable when fed oats. For this reason, oats are seldom fed to ponies.

Maize

a. Whole maize is too hard and indigestible to feed. It is fed in a cooked, flaked form.

b. A good sample will consist of large firm flakes, yellow and white in colour. It should not be dusty, grey nor smell mouldy.

c. Maize is high in energy and inclined to be fattening. It makes some horses overly excitable.

Sugar Beet

a. This product comes in dried and shredded or cubed form and must be soaked before it can be fed to horses. The shreds should be soaked overnight. Fill the container half full with shreds then fill almost to the top with cold water. The cubes should be soaked for longer, up to 24 hours, and require more water. Fill the selected receptacle one-third full of cubes and almost to the top with cold water.

b. Sugar beet is high in fibre and provides the horse with a moderate amount of energy. It is a succulent and tasty addition to the diet.

c. A good sample will be sweet smelling, dark grey in colour and dry without being dusty.

Cubes (Horse and Pony/Event/Stud/Complete, etc.)

a. There are many different types of cube, each formulated as a balanced diet for horses and ponies in a particular type of work. For this reason, nutrient levels and energy values will vary.

b. They provide horses with a good balance of nutrients, helping to make sure that nothing is lacking in the diet.

c. A good sample should be dry so that each cube will break but not crumble.

Coarse Mixes

a. As with cubes, there are many different types, each formulated to provide the right balance of nutrients to horses and ponies in different types of work.

b. The mix often contains molasses, which makes a moist and tasty feed which most horses enjoy.

c. Good samples will be sweet and fresh smelling, with no traces of mould or dust.

d. Like cubes, they provide a good balance of nutrients and are convenient to feed as there is no need to add any other concentrates to the ration.

Chaff

a. This is chopped hay or straw. You can make the chaff yourself, although it can be bought in molassed form which is very popular as a tasty addition to feed.

b. It is added to the concentrate ration to encourage the horse to chew the feed thoroughly. It will help to slow down the type of horse that bolts its feed, and also adds fibre to the diet.

Bran

a. This is a by-product, left over after the milling process of wheat.
b. It is a high-fibre feed and will absorb water easily.
c. It is most useful when made into a bran mash, which can be fed as part of a laxative diet: 500 g–1 kg (1–2 lb) of bran is placed in a bucket. Add boiling water and mix until the consistency is crumbly, not sloppy. Cover with a cloth and leave to cool and steam through. (A tablespoon of salt/handful of oats/Epsom salts, etc., may be added as required.) Feed while still warm.
d. As bran is quite expensive and low in calcium while being high in phosphorus (which is not a good balance for horses), it should only be fed in small quantities, mixed with the rest of the horse's ration, or as a bran mash.
e. When water is added to dampen the feed, it is absorbed by the bran. This helps to create a moist, palatable mix for the horse. These days, however, mollichaff is often used instead of bran for the reasons given in (d).

Linseed

a. Linseed is a small, shiny, dark brown seed that comes from the flax plant.
b. It must be cooked before being fed to horses in order to destroy an enzyme that produces poisonous cyanide. Place approximately 500g (1 lb) of linseed in a large saucepan. Soak the linseed overnight in approximately 8–10 cm (3–4 in) of water. Bring to the boil and then simmer for several hours. Add water if necessary, as much of the water will simmer away during cooking. You should end up with an oily jelly that can be added to the normal feed or to a bran mash.
c. The oil content of the seed helps to add a shine to the horse's coat and generally improves condition.

Succulents

a. The addition of succulents to the diet adds interest, makes the feed more tempting and palatable and provides a useful source of a variety of vitamins.

b. Carrots are most frequently fed and should always be cut lengthways. Small circles of carrot could become lodged in the oesophagus and cause choking.

c. Apples are usually relished and should be cut into quarters. Do not feed more than two or three at a time.

d. Swedes can be fed whole and left in the horse's manger for it to chew on.

4. Deciding What to Feed

Each horse has very individual requirements. We all know that some humans seem to get fat easily while others always seem to be thin. Also, that some are allergic to various foods and others become hyperactive on

A horse being weighed on a weighbridge

caffeine or other substances. Horses have similar problems, which means a suitable diet for one horse may not be suitable for another. To formulate a ration, start by following some basic guidelines, then be prepared to alter the diet according to how the horse looks, behaves and performs.

Estimating the Horse's Total Daily Feed Requirements

a. A horse's appetite is equal to approximately 2.5 per cent of its body weight.
b. The ideal way to check the horse's body weight is to weigh it on a weighbridge. If you do not have access to one of these, the weight can be estimated using a weight tape or by referring to a weight chart.

Using a weight tape to estimate the weight of a horse

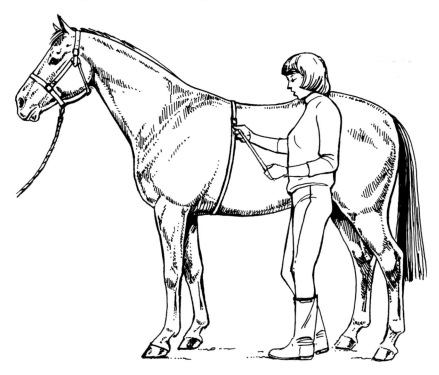

c. The following heights and weights can be used as guidelines (but
    are only approximate).

12 h.h.	230–280 kg	(506–616 lb)
13 h.h.	280–350 kg	(616–770 lb)
14 h.h.	350–420 kg	(770–924 lb)
15 h.h.	420–520 kg	(924–1,144 lb)
16 h.h.	500–600 kg	(1,100–1,320 lb)

d. To work out a daily feed ration for a 16 h.h. horse which weighs
    520 kg (1,144 lb), divide the body weight by 100 and then multi-
    ply by 2.5. Thus, 520 divided by 100x2.5 = 13. This figure is the
    horse's appetite in kilograms (13 kg or $28^1/_2$ lb) of dry matter per
    day. The horse should be fed a little below this amount in order
    not to overfeed. (NB: 1 kg = 2.2 lb.)
e. This total daily feed intake of the horse will be split into the
    hay/haylage/grass ration and its concentrate ration. The follow-
    ing percentages can be used as guidelines (but, again, are only
    approximate).

	% hay/haylage/grass ration	% concentrate
Resting horse	100	
Light work	75	25
Medium work	60	40
Hard work	40–50	50–60

f. If the horse on 13 kg ($28^1/_2$ lb) of feed per day is in medium work,
    it could have 7.8–8 kg (17–18 lb) of hay and 5–5.2 kg (11–12 lb) of
    concentrates.

Selecting the Right Type of Feed

a. Weigh out the horse's ration rather than giving random scoop-
    fuls. Each scoopful will vary according to whether it is heaped or
    level.
b. It is always safer to give a horse a low concentrate and high fibre
    ration. If in doubt, give plenty of soaked hay (weigh the hay

ration before soaking) and small amounts of concentrates at first. If the horse is well behaved, looking well, working well and happy in itself, then there is no need to alter this balance of feed.

c. If the horse is too energetic and silly, the concentrate ration should be cut down and more hay given. If it is lethargic and struggling to do the work asked, despite a progressive fitness programme, it probably needs more concentrate and less hay.

d. Use low energy feeds for horses in light work, for example horse and pony nuts, non-heating coarse mix, sugar beet.

e. Give sick and resting horses a laxative diet of sugar beet and chaff, or bran mashes, and plenty of soaked hay.

f. Old horses need easily digested feeds such as micronised or boiled barley, or coarse mix.

g. Horses with respiratory problems may need haylage rather than soaked hay. As haylage is very nutritious, the concentrate ration may have to be cut back to avoid the horse receiving overly large amounts of high-energy feed.

h. If your horse tends to bolt its feed, place a salt or mineral block in its manger. Having to eat around this will slow it down. It will also have the salt and minerals available to lick as required. A whole swede could be used for this purpose too or large whole carrots.

i. For those owners with one or two horses, using coarse mix or cubes and chaff will eliminate the need to buy several bags of different feeds, which can lead to waste.

j. Larger yards may buy oats, barley, cubes, sugar beet and chaff to cater for the needs of a wider variety of horses in different work.

k. As work is gradually increased during a fitness programme, the concentrates should also be increased while the hay ration is decreased.

l. As the concentrate ration is increased, it should be divided into several small feeds. Three or four feeds a day usually fit well into the work routine. Concentrates of 2–2.5 kg (4–6 lb) should be considered the maximum amount per feed in order not to overload the stomach. More than this may not be efficiently digested.

m. Having decided on a feed ration, make a chart in the feed room. Write up the quantities and types of feed to be given to each horse; this will ensure that a horse's diet is not changed suddenly if different people feed the horse from time to time. Keep the feed chart up to date. All changes must be made gradually.

Follow-up Work to Confirm Knowledge and Experience

1. When visiting different yards or trade stands at shows, look at all the different types of feed on offer to help you to become familiar with a wide range of feedstuffs.
2. Find out about feeding programmes in use with any horses you come across. Compare how different people feed horses of various sizes and types in different types of work. Look at these horses and their performance records to help you to decide if their feed programmes have been well worked out.

Helpful Hints and Exam Technique

In an exam situation candidates often come to grief when describing how much concentrate and hay they will feed a variety of horses. This is mainly caused by not relating what they actually feed to horses on a day-to-day basis to a quantity they can describe in words. It is vital that students practise weighing out quantities of all different types of feed, including hay and haylage. If students only give feeds that have been measured out for them, they may develop a good eye for the right quantity but how will they describe that quantity to their examiner?

Another common mistake is to refer to quantities required by the horse as percentages but then to be unable to work out the mathematics to convert these percentages into actual amounts of feed. Don't use this process if you cannot follow it through! You need to be able to express amounts in pounds or kilograms, it doesn't matter which, so some basic mathematical ability is required. For example, if you think a horse needs 12.7 kg (28 lb) of feed a day and half of that should be hay, then the horse will receive 6.3 kg (14 lb) of hay and 6.3 kg (14 lb) of concentrate. You then need to be able to divide the 6.3 kg (14 lb) of concentrates into three or four feeds. Three feeds of 1.8–2.3 kg (4–5 lb) is accurate enough.

5 Fitness Work / Preparation / Roughing Off / Different Disciplines

By working horses progressively and following a programme suited to the aims for that horse, we can keep horses healthy and sound in wind and limb while working them at the level required.

1. Bringing a Horse Up from Grass/Rest

An event horse will usually have a winter break and a hunter a summer break. An injured horse will be forced to rest during the healing of the injury and some horses may simply have a break when their owners go on holiday.

The time of year and type of rest period will influence the procedure to be followed in order to prepare the horse for work again. A summer holiday at grass means that the horse is likely to be a little overweight and in soft condition. However, its muscles, tendons and ligaments will be firmer than those of a horse that has been confined to box rest because of injury. Horses on winter holidays will have been given concentrate feeds and hay to make up for a lack of grazing, while horses on summer grazing will have to be reintroduced to this type of feed.

    a. Prior to starting the fitness programme, arrange for the vet to give any vaccinations due, for example, flu and tetanus. The vet can also recommend what type of wormer you should dose your horse with at this stage.

    b. Either the vet or a horse dentist should check the horse's teeth.

    c. Contact the farrier and have the horse shod. Stud holes may be needed from the beginning so that road studs can be used.

    d. Order feed, hay/haylage and bedding.

    e. Check that your stables are clean and in good repair.

f. Check that all your tack, rugs and accessories are clean, repaired where necessary and ready to use.

g. The horse that has been at grass should be brought into its stable for a short period each day. This will help it to adjust to standing in again. It can gradually be kept in for longer and longer periods. As it has been in a fresh outdoor environment, take care to keep the stable well ventilated and free from dust in order to avoid respiratory problems.

h. While standing in, the horse can also gradually be reintroduced to concentrate feed and hay. Start with small amounts, damp the feed and soak the hay.

i. Horses on winter holidays will probably have been stabled at night and are therefore already accustomed to points (g) and (h) above.

j. Begin grooming as it will take some time to clean all the grease from the coat, especially if the horse has a winter coat which you will need to clip in a few weeks' time. Do not clip until the horse has completed one or two weeks of its fitness programme. It will need its coat to keep it warm while it is only at the walking stage.

k. The mane and tail can gradually be pulled and the feathers trimmed.

l. Rub surgical spirit into areas of soft skin that need to be hardened ready to take the girth, saddle and bridle.

m. Introduce light rugs. This will help to improve the coat if you are coming into the summer months, and will prepare the horse for heavier rugs if you are heading for winter.

n. Finally, if you are hunting or competing, make sure you have paid your subscription, membership or entry fees.

2. The Fitness Programme

a. With the horse in a correct outline, steady and purposeful walking on firm ground will tone up muscles, tendons and ligaments, making them strong and ready for the work to follow. As work progresses, the efficiency of the heart and lungs will gradually improve.

b. Horses that are recovering from injury need a slow beginning to their fitness programme, with many weeks of walking. And if recovering from tendon/ligament injury, they may need anything from four to eight weeks or even more, depending on the severity of the injury. Your vet will advise you.

c. Mature, experienced horses will need one to two weeks of walking. Start with half an hour and increase the time each day until you are walking for one to one and a half hours.

d. Always be aware of the type of ground you are working on. Soft, deep going will pull and strain tendons/muscles, especially when the horse is still in soft condition. A horse is also likely to overreach when its feet are held by deep mud.

Knee boots. These boots are fitted to protect the horse in case it slips up when being ridden on the road

e. Only walk, or trot very gently, for short periods when on hard ground and roads. The concussion created when the horse's hooves meet the hard ground can lead to strain and inflammation. Roads are also very slippery, which means that trotting can be dangerous.

f. Stony ground can cause bruised soles and uneven ground may cause a slip or trip, leading to strains.

g. Although lungeing is a strenuous activity, generally used when the horse is fairly fit, it may be necessary to lunge a very fresh horse before you ride it. Some horses take time to settle into the working routine. If they are inclined to buck and generally misbehave, it will be safer to lunge them for 10–15 minutes first.

h. Continue to turn your horse out whenever possible. Providing it does not have access to large amounts of grass, is not inclined to pace the fence line or gallop about and appears content, it will benefit from the fresh air and space to move. Horses confined to the stable for 20 or more hours a day are likely to stiffen up, suffer from circulatory problems and develop stable vices.

Lungeing the horse. (Note that the lunger is not correctly dressed for this task. He should be wearing a hard hat.)

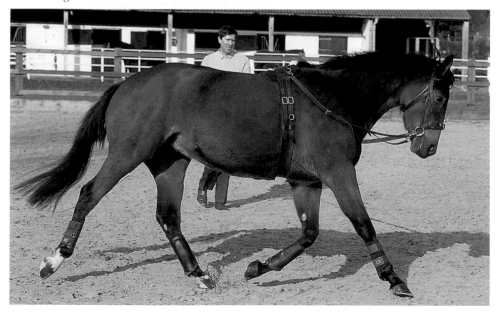

i.   The best way to increase fitness without increasing concussion is to introduce hillwork. Start with gentle slopes, then gradually work up steeper and longer hills each day. Providing the horse is kept in a good outline, it will really have to use its topline muscles. Also, the greater effort required for walking or trotting uphill will make the horse physically stronger while developing the efficiency of its heart and lungs.

j.   Each rider's routine will vary according to where they live. Some may have to cover many miles of road to reach good riding country, while others may have easy access to woodland, hills, etc. It may be necessary to travel by horse box to a good area for cantering or hillwork. This can be good practice for younger horses, teaching them to enjoy travelling and remain relaxed.

k.   Throughout the programme, observe your horse's respiratory rate, making sure its breathing quickly returns to normal after any period of work. If not, you are doing too much work too soon. Check the horse's legs, which should be cool, firm and free from swelling. Any deviation from normal may indicate that you have progressed to fast work too quickly or that you are over-feeding concentrate feed.

Always work the horse in a good outline when riding out. For building top-line muscles, hill work is particularly beneficial

l. All being well, introduce trotting into your daily programme. Start with approximately one minute, preferably on a gentle upward slope. Include two to four short trots spaced out over the one to one and a half hours' work. Each day, the length of time spent in trot can be gradually increased. Again, avoid concussion by using slopes and hills where possible.

m. In the early stages of the programme, some riders will not give their horse a day off. They may just ride it gently for a short period so that it has an easier day. This routine is helpful if you have limited turning out facilities, although most riders work their horses for six days a week and give one complete rest day.

n. Once the trotting phase has been well established over a period of two to three weeks, canter work can be introduced in exactly the same way. Keep the canter steady, with the horse working in a good outline.

o. Always make sure the horse is well warmed up before trotting or cantering. A purposeful walk for at least a quarter of an hour is essential for loosening and warming up the muscles, especially if the horse has come straight out of the stable.

p. Either just before, or just after, canter work has been introduced, work in the school can be included. Excitable horses may be calmer about having their first short canter in the school rather than out in the woods.

q. Start with 15–20 minutes' school work, using mainly walk and trot and keeping to large circles and simple movements. Gradually increase the school work according to your horse's needs. (An event horse will need more than a hunter, for example.) Some horses will work and concentrate better if you go straight into school work before hacking out to do your fitness work. Most horses will benefit from the warming-up and the loosening-up effect of the fitness work prior to going into the school.

r. At this stage you may start to split the work up into two sessions. The horse may be working from one to two and a half hours a day, depending upon the type of work done. More intensive work in the school will result in a shorter working session, while steady walk and trot work will mean longer sessions.

s. Introduce show jumping and cross country practice as necessary once you have built up the schooling over a period of one or two weeks.

t. In general, a week's work will follow a pattern that includes a regular rest day, schooling and jumping once or twice a week and basic fitness work on the days between. Some horses will benefit from a short schooling session every day.

- With the horse in a correct outline, steady and purposeful walking on firm ground, will tone up muscles, tendons, and ligaments

u. In the last two to three weeks of the programme, those horses that will be doing fast work (hunters, eventers, etc.) will need to do some more purposeful canter work, followed by a "pipe opener". Select a suitable stretch of field where you can canter steadily for one to two minutes, then gently move the horse on to approximately 20–30 seconds of gallop, followed by gradually returning to walk. Never pull up quickly and always finish with a long period of walk while the horse gradually recovers its normal respiratory rate. If your build-up work has been correct, it should recover within two to five minutes.

v. An experienced hunter will need a six to eight week programme. Cub hunting will then help to prepare the horse for a full day's hunting. A novice event horse will need 10–12 weeks to prepare for its first Novice event, and a more advanced event horse will need approximately 16 weeks.

w. The ratio of concentrate to bulk feed will gradually change during the programme. Start with approximately 70 per cent bulk and 30 per cent concentrate. Each week the bulk can be lowered and the concentrate increased, until you finish up with approximately 40–50 per cent bulk and 50–60 per cent concentrate.

3. Associated Ailments

Ailments most commonly associated with fitness work include:

a. Respiratory problems brought about by being stabled in a poorly ventilated environment, and by being fed hay contaminated with mould spores.

b. Strains to muscles, tendons and ligaments due to working an unfit horse too hard too quickly.

c. Bruised soles from trotting or cantering over uneven or stony ground.

d. Galls caused by tack that may be dirty or ill fitting, rubbing against soft skin.

e. Overreach wounds brought about by the horse working in an unbalanced manner or moving too fast through deep going.

f. Bruising and inflammation from the effects of concussion, brought about by working too fast on roads and very hard ground.

All of the above can be avoided through good management and progressive ridden work. The unavoidable does happen, however. For example, a setback may be caused by the horse treading on a stone while out in the field, resulting in a bruised sole. The fitness programme may then need to be extended by one or two weeks. Allow for this when planning your first competition. Count back the required number of weeks from the competition date to the start of the fitness programme, then go back one or two more weeks to allow for injury.

4. Care after Hard Work

On return from hunting, eventing or other strenuous activity, the horse will need special attention. It needs to be made comfortable so that it can rest while its systems return to normal. At the same time, being tired, it will benefit from the minimum of fuss.

a. Try to return home with a cool, dry horse. If it is wet, warm and sweaty, it will need to be walked in hand until dry and cool. Some stables may be equipped with infra-red lamps for drying horses. Whichever method is used, the first priority is to get the horse dry but not to allow it to become chilled.

b. In some areas of the country horses return from hunting so caked in mud and clay that the only solution is to bath them immediately. A supply of warm water, shampoo and a washing-down area out of the wind are required. The bathing/rinsing process should be quick and thorough. Again, the first priority is to keep the horse warm and get it dry as quickly as possible.

c. The horse may be thirsty but should not be allowed to drink large amounts of cold water. Add a small amount of hot water to a bucket of cold water (just enough to take the chill off). Offer water to the horse every 5–10 minutes, allowing it to drink only 2 or 3 litres (4 or 6 pt) at a time. Once it has quenched its thirst, it can be left with a normal supply of water.

d. Any obvious wounds should have been noticed and dealt with accordingly. The horse now needs to be carefully checked for any hidden cuts, bruises or swellings. Early discovery and attention will aid a quick recovery.

e. The horse should have a deep, warm bed and be rugged with light, warm rugs suitable for the time of year. A tired horse will often feel the cold more. Stable bandages will keep its extremities warm, at the same time giving support to tired limbs.

f. If the horse was not bathed, a light grooming will remove enough dried mud and dried sweat to make it comfortable. Always pick out the feet.

g. Feed the usual hay ration and also a light, easily digested concentrate feed. A bran mash with linseed would be warming and enjoyable.

h. Having settled the horse, return at intervals to check its behaviour. Some horses break out in a secondary sweat and will need to be walked and dried again. Others may suffer a colic attack. Hourly checks should be sufficient unless you suspect a problem, in which case check every 15–20 minutes.

i. The following day, the horse may be stiff or even lame. It should be led out in hand to help it loosen up. Then trot it up to check for soundness. All being well, it will benefit from a day in the field where it can rest but also gently exercise its tired muscles.

5. Roughing Off

After a season of hard work, most horses will need a rest. This may be a complete rest, turned out to grass 24 hours a day, or a period of gentle activity, perhaps partly stabled and ridden out for an enjoyable hack most days.

a. Begin by reducing the concentrate ration and increasing the bulk.

b. Reduce the amount of exercise gradually. (Stop schooling, jumping and fast work straightaway.)

c. If the horse is having a winter break in the field, allow its coat, mane and tail to grow for warmth and protection. (It may need a New Zealand rug.) Also groom less so that grease returns to the coat to make it waterproof.

d. Reduce the number or thickness of rugs worn. This will encourage the coat to grow.

• After hunting, eventing, or other strenuous activity, give your horse special attention. Check for injuries, wash it down, give water in small amounts, keep it warm, check feet and shoes, and be alert to anything unusual

e. Begin turning the horse out in the field for longer periods. This process should be gradual if the horse has not had access to much grass and is now going to have a summer holiday.

f. If vaccinations, worming or tooth rasping are due soon, now is a good time.

g. If the horse is not going to be ridden, you may have all or just the hind shoes removed.

h. For those horses that will be staying out at night, pick the best possible weather for their first night out.

i. If the horse has not been turned out daily during its working season, it is likely to be very excitable when first let loose. Ride it first to make it a little tired, put brushing boots on all four legs for protection and turn it out hungry so that it is keen to settle and eat the grass.

j. This whole process will take approximately two weeks.

6. Lungeing

a. Another alternative to ridden exercise is lungeing. Although this is a fairly strenuous activity, it may be necessary to lunge a fresh horse prior to riding in order to settle it into a more sensible frame of mind.

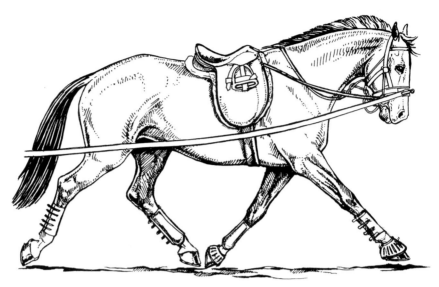

A horse equipped for lungeing

b. Once the horse is fit, or partly so, it is a useful way of varying the exercise routine and improving suppleness and discipline.

c. Twenty minutes' active work on the lunge can be equal to one hour's ridden work. It is important, therefore, to start with just five or ten minutes and build up gradually, as with all fitness work.

d. Too often, horses are put on the end of a lunge line with no tack other than the lunge cavesson or a head collar, and then are just allowed to trot and canter round as they please. This is not a beneficial form of exercise and will not improve the horse's way of going. It is merely a way of letting the horse stretch its legs.

e. To be exercised and improved in its fitness and way of going, the horse needs to be tacked up and worked by the lunger just as if he or she were actually riding it.

f. Firstly, when the horse is sent out on to the circle, obedience should be considered. Unless the horse is so fresh that it is likely to kick and buck, putting the lunger at risk, it should be asked to walk out on to the circle, moving away from the lunger calmly. If you were riding the horse, you would not tolerate it trotting away the minute you sat in the saddle, so, in the same way, you do not tolerate it rushing off into trot the minute you let it out on the lunge. However, for the sake of safety, you may need to let a very fresh horse move off quickly, then bring it back to walk and start again when it is in a calmer frame of mind and ready to pay attention.

g. As the person lungeing, you should never back away from the horse as this only encourages the horse to come towards you, causing a loss of control. You should walk forward with the horse, keeping level with its shoulder, and gradually let the horse move away from you, encouraging it to do so with voice and lunge whip. In fact, if the horse does fall in or come towards you, you should move towards it, at the same time pushing it forward more. This will encourage it to go forward and out on to a larger circle.

h. While sending the horse out on the circle, it is essential to keep a good steady contact on the lunge line. Each time you lose contact you are losing control.

i. Once the horse is on the circle, maintain contact with the lunge line and keep yourself positioned opposite, or just behind, the horse's shoulder, with the lunge whip pointing towards the horse's hindquarters. Your body should form the apex of a triangle with the horse's body as the base and the lunge line and whip the other two sides.

j. Using your voice, backed up by the whip as necessary, you give commands to the horse. Just as, when you ride the horse, you give aids to prepare for different movements and transitions, so, now, you use your voice to prepare the horse on the lunge. For example: (the preparation) "Dobbin, aaand" (the command) "Terrrot". Using the horse's name is a good way of gaining its attention. Keep commands simple and consistent to avoid confusion.

k. The horse should be worked actively forward into a contact with the side reins (which may be attached once the horse has worked in), in a good outline, being asked to track up in trot and remain steady and balanced in canter. The walk isn't used so much as, once the side reins are adjusted for trot and canter work, they will be too short for walk and therefore restrictive.

l. The size of the circle used can be varied but remember that constant circle work is strenuous and it is preferable to keep the circle at around 18–20 m. As the lunger, you can walk a small circle in the middle but be careful not to wander as the horse may catch you off balance or you may encourage crookedness or a lack of balance in the horse.

m. The lunger needs to practise standing and moving in a balanced way. For example, when lungeing on the left rein, the right leg should step forward and around the left leg, and vice versa on the right rein. If you remain in balance, you can move with the horse easily if it pulls or shoots off, or you can stand your ground if the horse gets strong. It is advisable to remove spurs before lungeing in case you trip yourself up!

n. You should also wear gloves for lungeing, to protect your hands and aid grip. It is advisable to wear a hard hat as young, fit or excited horses can easily fly-buck and kick out at head height.

o. Practice is needed in handling the lunge line and whip. The line should be kept smooth and evenly coiled. Avoid long loops of line that may catch around your feet and trip you up, and also avoid having small loops around your hand which can quickly tighten and trap you if the horse suddenly pulls. If the line is kept straight and not twisted, then it can be smoothly let out or coiled in and a good contact can be maintained. The whip should be kept tucked under your arm facing behind you when you are close to the horse, adjusting tack, etc., and should be passed round behind you when changing hands, otherwise the horse may think you are waving the whip at it. Do not put the whip on the ground if you can possibly avoid it, as when you bend down to pick it up, the horse can easily take fright or take advantage of the situation and get out of control. When using the whip, keep it pointing slightly downwards, towards the horse's hocks, and swing it forward so that it follows up behind the horse.

p. The key to effective lungeing is to treat it like riding the horse. You are simply using a different set of aids but are looking for the same qualities in the horse's work. The horse should go freely and actively forward, keeping a rhythm and remaining straight and balanced in a good outline.

q. If you intend to lunge the horse and then continue its work by riding it, use its normal tack but make sure you put brushing boots on all four legs as, when working continuously on a circle, and possibly putting in an occasional buck or losing balance, the horse can easily knock into itself. Secure the stirrup irons by looping them up in the leathers, and secure the reins by twisting them and looping the throatlatch through them. Attach side reins so that you will have a contact to work the horse into, and use a lunge cavesson for control. Sometimes overreach boots are used for protection on young, unbalanced or particularly boisterous horses.

r. If you do not intend to ride the horse then a lungeing roller can be used instead of a saddle to attach the side reins to. You could also remove the noseband from the bridle to help the lunge cavesson to sit more comfortably.

s. When carried out effectively, lungeing is an excellent way of improving the horse's level of fitness throughout the training programme. It is also a helpful way of maintaining fitness and can be used as an alternative form of exercise from time to time. As with ride and lead, there may be occasions when a horse cannot be ridden but can be lunged, for example if it cannot wear a saddle or if it hasn't yet been backed!

Follow-up Work to Confirm Knowledge and Experience

1. Being involved in the fitness programmes of as many different horses as possible is the best way to gain experience in this area.
2. Practise lungeing frequently, with as many different horses and ponies as possible. This is the only way to become effective at the job.

Helpful Hints and Exam Technique

 Candidates often make the mistake of learning a basic fitness programme for a hunter then cannot adjust to describe how they would work a horse that simply needed to be fit enough for general hacking. If they really had some experience, they would be aware that the first three or four weeks of the hunter fitness programme would produce a horse fit enough for hacking.

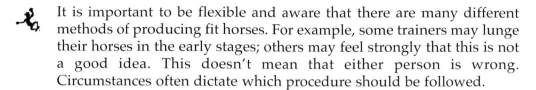

It is important to be flexible and aware that there are many different methods of producing fit horses. For example, some trainers may lunge their horses in the early stages; others may feel strongly that this is not a good idea. This doesn't mean that either person is wrong. Circumstances often dictate which procedure should be followed.

Try to speak from your own experience. All horses need to be fit for their jobs, so think about the work your own horse or the horses you take care of do. Don't try to invent something that is beyond your own experience.

6 Saddlery, Its Use, Care and Fitting for Riding, Training and Competition

For horse and rider to work safely and in harmony, it is essential to select the right tack for the job in mind, to be able to fit it correctly and to be able to check it is in safe condition for use.

1. Fitting the Equipment

GP Saddle

The tree, around which the saddle is built, is made in various widths, usually narrow, medium and wide. Saddles are also made with different lengths of seat to accommodate various sizes of rider. The saddle should be fitted without a numnah then girthed up with the horse standing level.

    a. When placed on the horse's back, there must be a clear passage down the gullet. No weight should be taken on the horse's spine.

    b. There should be approximately 10 cm (4 in) clearance between the pommel and the withers, without the rider.

    c. The saddle should be level, neither too low at the front nor at the back, which would tip the rider forwards or backwards.

    d. The full surface of the panels should be in contact with the horse's back. These will distribute the rider's weight over the largest possible area.

    e. The length of the saddle should suit the length of the horse's back. There should not be any weight on the loins.

    f. The knee roll, panels and saddle flap should not protrude over the shoulder, as they may restrict the horse's freedom of movement.

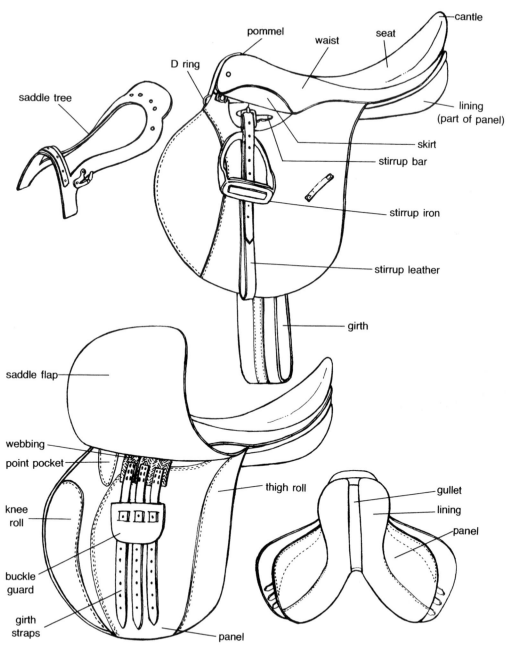

The points of the saddle

g. The fitting of the saddle is not complete until seen with the rider on top. The rider's weight will reduce the amount of clearance over the withers and spine.

Snaffle Bridle

Bridles are made in different sizes: pony, cob and full size. There are also different widths and strengths of leather. For example, bridles for heavy-weight horses and hunters will be made of strong, broad strips of leather, while bridles for show ponies will be made from finer leather.

a. The purpose of the browband is to keep the headpiece from slipping back down the horse's neck. It should not pull the

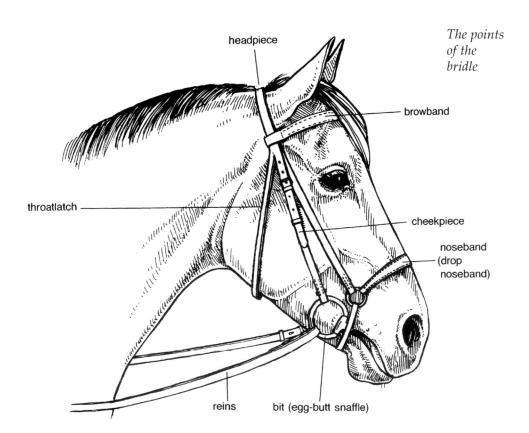

headpiece

The points of the bridle

browband

throatlatch

cheekpiece

noseband (drop noseband)

reins   bit (egg-butt snaffle)

*Checking the
space under
the saddle*

*A well-fitting
bridle and GP
saddle*

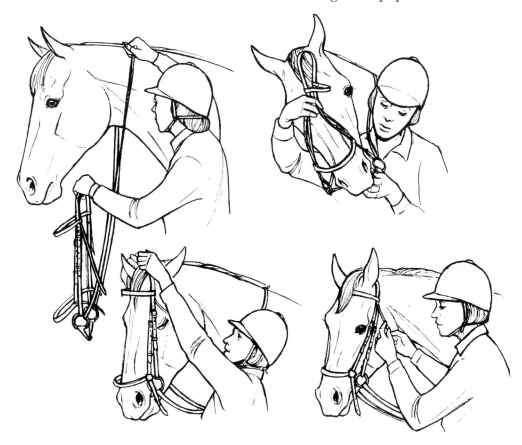

The correct procedure for putting on the bridle

headpiece forward where it will rub, but should keep it in place just behind the ears.

b. The throatlatch, which is attached to the headpiece, prevents the bridle being pulled off over the horse's ears. It should not be tight when the horse flexes at the poll. When it is correctly adjusted, you should be able to fit the width of your hand between the horse's cheek and the throatlatch.

c. Apart from having the throatlatch attached to it, the headpiece also supports the cheekpieces.

d. The cheekpieces support the bit and should be long or short enough to enable you to adjust the bit to the correct level.

e. The reins are attached to the bit to give the rider control. They should not be too short, which may cause the rider to let go if the horse suddenly snatches its head down, nor should they be too long which may lead to the reins becoming tangled around the rider's foot.

f. The cavesson noseband is a point of attachment for a standing martingale. However, it is often worn just to make the bridle look complete. It should sit the width of two fingers below the projecting cheek bones and be loose around the nose to allow free movement of the jaws. Allow for the width of two fingers between the front of the horse's nose and the noseband.

g. The snaffle bit should be adjusted to a height where it wrinkles the corners of the horse's mouth. The mouthpiece should not protrude more than 6 mm ($^1/_4$ in) on either side of the horse's mouth, nor should the bit rings appear to pinch inwards. If the bit is too wide, it will slide from side to side when the rider uses the reins. If it is too narrow, it will pinch and rub the sides of the mouth.

Martingales

a. The neck straps of both the standing and running martingale should fit around the base of the neck, allowing for the width of one hand to be placed between the neck and the neck strap.

b. To fit the standing martingale, place the neck strap over the horse's head and attach one end to the girth. Then follow the line of the underside of the horse's neck with the martingale strap, up under its throat and down to its chin groove.

c. To fit the running martingale, place the strap over the horse's neck and attach the end to the

- For horse and rider to work safely and in harmony it is essential to select the right tack for the job and to make sure it is correctly fitted. Badly fitted, or poorly selected, tack will prove detrimental to the horse's performance

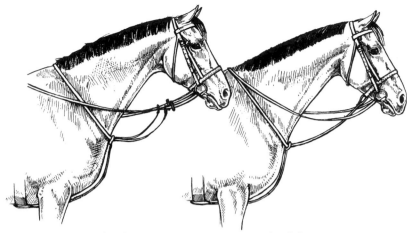

The fitting of accessories: (left) *running martingale and* (right) *standing martingale*

girth. If both rings are drawn back along the line of the shoulder, they should be approximately 15–20 cm (6–8 in) short of reaching the withers.

d. Rein stops must be worn with the running martingale. They will prevent the rings from becoming stuck where the reins buckle on to the bit.

e. Both martingales will prevent the horse from raising its head too high: the standing type by exerting pressure on the nose via the cavesson noseband; the running type by exerting pressure on the reins, which is then transferred to the bit.

f. The running martingale will only work if the rider has a contact on the reins.

g. Provided they are correctly adjusted, both types of martingale should allow the horse free movement of the head and neck while working on the flat or over fences. They should only come into action when the horse tries to raise its head too high for the rider to maintain control.

Breastplate and Breastgirth

a. Both hunting- and racing-style breastplates and breastgirths should fit securely in order to fulfil their purpose of preventing the saddle from slipping back.

Two kinds of breastplate: (near right) breastgirth, or racing, breastplate and (far right) hunting breastplate

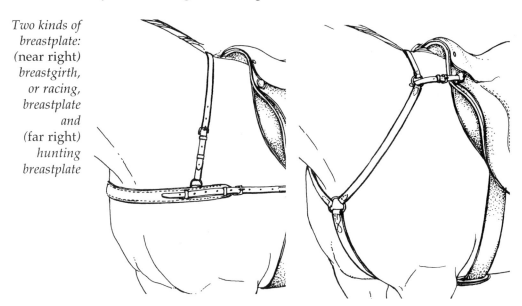

b. Allow for the width of your hand, on edge with thumb at top, between the withers and the wither/neck strap of both styles.

c. The racing style should fit close to the chest without restricting the shoulder movement.

d. The hunting style should follow the line of the horse's shoulder blades, with the centre ring sitting at the base of the neck in the middle of the chest.

e. The strap from the chest to the girth should hang some 3–6 cm (1–1$^{1}/_{2}$ in) below the horse's chest.

f. A running or standing martingale attachment can be used with the hunting-style breastplate and with some designs of racing breastgirths. Simply attach and then fit in the same way as described for the martingales.

Lunge Cavesson

a. Because of the force exerted on the lunge cavesson by the lunge line, it must be fitted firmly, hence the need for plenty of padding around the nosepiece.

b. The headpiece and browband (which is optional) should fit as described for the snaffle bridle.

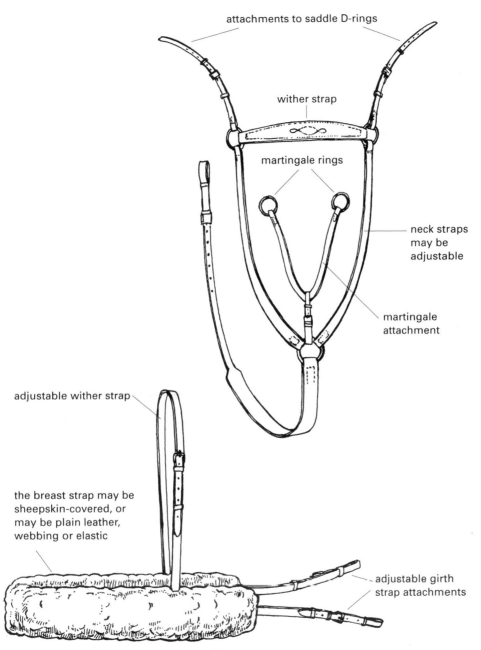

attachments to saddle D-rings

wither strap

martingale rings

neck straps
may be
adjustable

martingale
attachment

adjustable wither strap

the breast strap may be
sheepskin-covered, or
may be plain leather,
webbing or elastic

adjustable girth
strap attachments

Here two types of breastplate/girth are illustrated: a hunting breastplate (top) *and* (bottom) *a racing breastplate*

c. The nosepiece should be fitted at the same height as a cavesson noseband (which is normally removed if the bridle is being worn), but should be firmly buckled, without pinching, to prevent the lunge cavesson from slipping.

d. The throatlatch, or jowl strap, which is fitted lower than on the snaffle bridle, is buckled firmly around the lower half of the horse's cheeks. It also helps to stop the lunge cavesson from slipping.

A horse equipped with a lunge cavesson

Lunge cavesson fitted with a snaffle bridle

e. If being used, the bridle should be put on first, with the lunge cavesson placed on top. Then put the throatlatch and nosepiece under the cheekpieces of the bridle. This prevents the lunge cavesson from interfering with the action of the bit.

Some designs of lunge cavesson may not fit under the bridle cheekpieces without pulling them out of line. In this case, place the throatlatch over the bridle and the nosepiece underneath.

If the noseband is removed from the bridle, there will be more room for the lunge cavesson to sit comfortably.

Side Reins

These come in various different, adjustable designs.

a. Attach the loop end on each side of the horse by slotting the

*The correct
way to
attach a side
rein to the
girth strap*

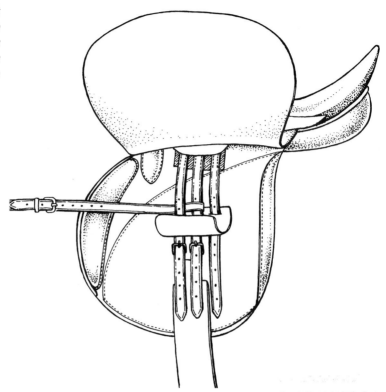

second or third girth strap through it. Then pass the side rein under first girth strap.

b. Once attached to the girth strap, hold each side rein in a straight line towards the horse's bit. While the horse is standing at rest with its head held in a relaxed position, the side reins should just reach the bit. This guideline gives a good starting point to work from. Subsequent adjustment depends on how the horse goes when worked on the lunge.

c. When not in use, the side reins can be hooked on to the D-rings of the saddle.

Boots

Boots come in many varied designs for different uses and are made from a variety of materials.

a. Some designs of boot currently available include:

- brushing boots – for general leg protection against knocks
- tendon boots – open-fronted to give support to the tendons, or not open to incorporate all-round leg protection with tendon support
- speedy cut boots – to protect horses with this action fault
- polo boots – thick felt boots to give all-round protection against the rigours of polo
- fetlock boots – to protect just this area
- sausage boots – to protect against low knocks round the coronet, or some designs are used in the stable to prevent capped elbow
- overreach boots – to protect the heels against overreaching.

The following general points will apply to the fitting of most boots.

a. The boot should not sit too high where it may rub the back of the

Some boot designs are illustrated here: (left) *simple brushing boots with Velcro fastenings;* (centre) *open-fronted tendon boots; and* (right) *leather brushing boots with buckle fastenings which provide tendon support and extra protection around the fetlock joint*

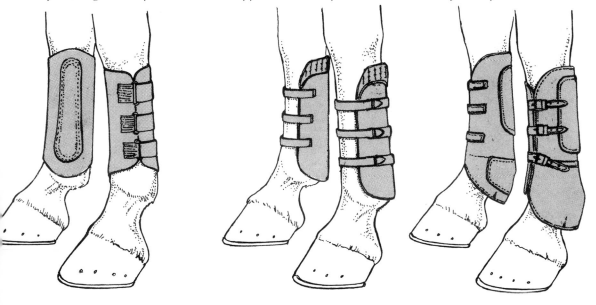

knee or front of the hock when the joint is flexed. It should not sit so low that it rubs the heels when the foot is moving.

b. A firm fit is required to prevent boots from slipping down the leg.

c. With most designs, straps are secured by being drawn firmly across the cannon bone and fastened pointing towards the rear. This helps to prevent unnecessary tension across the tendons.

d. To make them easy to put on and take off, boots are fastened on the outside of the leg. This also helps to prevent knocks against the opposite limb.

e. Fasten the centre strap first to secure the boot. If the horse begins to fidget before the other straps are fastened, the boot will then remain in place.

f. Likewise, if the centre strap is unfastened last, the boot will not slip if the horse fidgets when it is taken off.

Points to Remember when Removing Tack

a. When removing the bridle, start by undoing the noseband. This is essential if a drop or flash noseband is used, due to its firm fitting. Then undo the throatlatch. Push the headpiece gently forward over the horse's ears. Lower the bridle slowly in order to allow the horse to drop the bit in its own time. If you pull the bridle away quickly, the bit could catch on the horse's teeth. The horse may then be nervous of having its bridle removed in future. Leave the reins round its neck until you have slipped on the head collar.

b. When removing the saddle, let the girth down gently. If it is dropped down, it will bang against the horse's legs and can cause injury as well as frightening the horse. Then lift the saddle up, slightly back and towards you. In this way you avoid pulling against the horse's spine, which would cause bruising and discomfort.

c. When returning from a long hack or a day's hunting, it is a good idea to dismount before reaching home and loosen your horse's girth a little. This allows the circulation under the saddle to return gradually and avoids a sudden rush of blood (and therefore congestion) to the saddle area.

d. Secure the horse, by buckling the head collar around its neck, before you remove the bridle, then slip the head collar on and tie up. Now remove saddle and boots. To remove a martingale, the girth needs to be undone. In this case, tie up with the head collar over the bridle and remove the saddle first.

2. Care of the Equipment

The Thorough Cleaning Process

a. Undo all the buckles and take the tack completely apart. This includes removing stirrups and leathers, girth, numnah, reins, bit, cheekpieces, etc.
b. The bit, stirrups and treads can be washed in warm water then dried.
c. Remove any grease on the leather. This can be done with a blunt knife if care is taken not to scratch the leather.
d. Using lukewarm water, make a sponge damp, not wet, and work it over all the leather until it is clean.
e. Next, use a damp sponge to apply a layer of saddle soap which should be worked well into the leather.
f. A matchstick or tooth pick makes a useful instrument with which to clean all the buckle holes that have become clogged with grease or soap.
g. The stirrups and other metalwork can be cleaned with metal polish. Do not apply metal polish to the bit.
h. Girths and numnahs made of washable fabric can usually be hand or machine washed.
i. Synthetic saddles are washed, using a stiff brush and lukewarm water, then left to dry.
j. This complete cleaning process should take place after the tack has been used a maximum of five to six times. For horses in regular work, this is usually once a week.

After Each Use

a. Always wash the bit to prevent an accumulation of dried saliva and food which would soon rub the horse's mouth.

b. Remove the girth and numnah, brush clean and leave to air.
c. If boots are worn, brush or wash clean and leave to air.
d. Slip the bridle straps out of their keepers and run down the stirrups. With a damp sponge, remove obvious grease, mud and sweat. Work in a layer of saddle soap.

Additional Points on Cleaning and Care

a. While cleaning the tack, keep a constant check on its condition and therefore its safety.
b. If the tack gets very wet, take it apart and leave it to dry. Clean with a damp sponge then apply a layer of leather dressing. This will replace the oil lost and make the leather more supple. When the dressing has soaked in, apply a layer of saddle soap.
c. New leather will become more supple if leather dressing is applied. All leather will benefit from an application of dressing three or four times a year.
d. Tack should be kept in a warm room. If the atmosphere is damp, the leather will become mouldy and will rot but if it is too warm and dry the leather will dry out and crack.

Checking the Tack for Safety

a. All of the stitching will weaken and rot eventually. At the first signs of weakness, the item concerned should be sent to the saddler for restitching.
b. On the saddle, keep a particularly close check on the stitching that attaches the girth straps to the webbing under the saddle flaps. It undergoes considerable strain and if it rots your girth will no longer be secure!
c. The stitching that secures the buckle of the stirrup leather also takes a lot of strain, as does the stitching on the girth. Check these each time you use them.
d. The girth straps are often stitched to two separate pieces of webbing. If your girth is buckled to the first strap (attached to the first webbing) and either of the second two straps (attached to the second webbing), you have more security should one webbing break. Check the webbing for signs of wear.

e. The vital areas on the bridle include the stitching at the buckle and bit ends of the reins and on the cheekpieces.

f. Another major area of wear occurs at all buckle holes. These sometimes stretch so much that one hole begins to run into another. This severely weakens the leather which will then break easily. This frequently occurs on the girth straps.

g. Where straps are always buckled in the same hole, the leather may begin to crack from being constantly bent.

3. Injuries from Dirty or Ill-fitting Tack

If tack is dirty or does not fit correctly, it will rub, causing galls and bruising. The most common sites of these injuries are:

- the girth area just behind the elbow
- on top of and on either side of the withers
- either side of the spine just under the back of the saddle
- behind the ears
- just under the projecting cheek bones
- the corners of the horse's mouth
- the chin groove

Treatment

a. Find and remove the cause.

b. Treat as a minor wound.

c. There are various ways in which the horse can be exercised while the wound is healing. Try ride and lead, use a bitless bridle or lunge.

Follow-up Work to Confirm Knowledge and Experience

1. There is no substitute for hands-on experience. Practise tacking up as many different horses and ponies as possible and check the fitting of tack in order to develop a good eye for fit.

2. Students at Stage Two and Three level should practise preparing horses for various competitions. All the better if they do so at a real competition where they will learn to become efficient and

cope with a horse that is likely to be unsettled and excited by its surroundings. Speed and efficiency are vital as few horses will stand quietly for long periods while someone fiddles with tack, bandages, etc.

Helpful Hints and Exam Technique

At Stages One and Two, candidates shouldn't worry if they come across an item of tack they are not familiar with. As long as they can make a sensible assessment of the item and work out what it is, the examiner will be happy as we don't expect candidates at this level to have experience of every item. They should, however, be familiar with items in common usage.

A good way of keeping up to date with new items on the market is to visit the local saddlery shop and have a good look at all the items on offer.

Before starting on a task set, have a good look at the horse you are working with to see if it is likely to need a narrow saddle or a small bridle, for example.

A common mistake made by candidates is not checking both sides of the equipment once they have fitted it to the horse. For example, they may put on a bridle and not realise that the noseband is sitting much higher on one side than the other, or that the cheekpieces are not adjusted to the same height on each side.

Always adjust tack to fit the horse. Candidates often put an item on, then tell the examiner it doesn't fit. If there are adjustment holes available, the examiner will then ask the candidate to adjust the item to fit. The candidate would give a much better impression if they had made these adjustments without being prompted.

7 Bitting

Learning about the structure of the horse's mouth and how various bits and nosebands work will help in the selection of appropriate bitting arrangements for a variety of horses.

1. Basic Principles

The following basic principles of bitting should enable you to assess the action of almost any type of bit. In general, we aim to school the horse in such a way that it will respond to the simplest form of bitting.

    a. There are five families of bits:

- snaffle
- curb
- Pelham
- gag
- bitless

All bits can be fitted into one of these categories:

    b. There are seven areas where pressure can be applied by various bits:

- tongue
- bars
- lips/corners of mouth
- nose
- poll
- chin groove
- roof of mouth (not used in modern day bitting)

    c. A thick mouthpiece will spread pressure over a larger surface area and will therefore be more gentle, whereas a thin mouthpiece will work in the opposite way and be more severe.

There are five families of bits. Some are illustrated on this and the opposite page.

Here (above, left) *is an English Hackamore and* (above, right) *a snaffle bridle with a snaffle bit with cheeks.*

The bridle (right) *is a double bridle which has two bits, a curb and a bridoon*

English gag-snaffle

A Pelham with curb chain and lip strap

d. Bits with loose rings or sliding mouthpieces give the bitting arrangement more mobility, while those with fixed mouthpieces and rings reduce the mobility. The horse's response will vary according to the bitting arrangement used.

• Where possible, ride a variety of horses in different types of bits and gain a first-hand feel of how they affect the horse and how you ride it

e. Bits with shanks – The longer the shank above the mouth-piece, the more leverage there is on the poll. The longer the shank below the mouthpiece, the more leverage on the bars.

f. A snaffle will apply pressure on the tongue, lips and bars of the horse's mouth.

Follow-up Work to Confirm Knowledge and Experience

1. To become familiar with a wide range of different bits, it may be necessary to visit the local saddlery shop and examine the range of bits available. Some of the yards which you visit or work at are bound to have a selection of bits but may not have a comprehensive range.

2. Where possible, ride a variety of horses in different types of bits and gain a first-hand feel of how they affect the horse and the way you ride it.

3. Fit as many different bits to as wide a range of horses as possible. A particular bit fitted to one horse with a particular type of mouth may look very different when fitted to another horse.

Helpful Hints and Exam Technique

Candidates are inclined to be muddled when describing the action of bits. Although you may think you understand the workings of the bit, it is important to practise talking about them in practical lesson sessions so that you know you can put your thoughts into words clearly.

8 Horse Clothing

The horse will benefit if the right clothing is selected for the occasion, and is correctly fitted and well cared for.

1. Rugs

Many different rug fastenings, materials and designs are used for every possible occasion. To check your horse's rug size, measure from the middle of its chest right around along its side to the point of its buttock. The rug is measured in a similar way: laid flat on the floor and measured from chest strap to the end of the rug.

To Rug Up

a. When putting the rug on, avoid throwing it over the horse, which may startle it, and aim to keep its hair lying flat. At the same time, take care to fold leg or surcingle straps over the rug to prevent them from swinging against the horse's legs and causing injury.

b. Fold the rug in half by bringing the tail end forward towards the wither end. Then place the folded rug well forward over the horse's withers. Unfold the rug and slide it back into place. It is best to leave it a little too far forward, as it will tend to slip back once the horse begins to move.

c. In general, it is best to fasten the roller or surcingles before the front straps. Some horses bite at the front of their rugs while the roller is being fastened and if the front strap is already buckled the horse could get its lower jaw caught in the front of the rug. Likewise, if the front strap is fastened first on a breezy day, the rug may blow forward and become tangled around the horse's front legs.

Rugging up using an underblanket

d. For the same reasons, undo the front strap first when removing the rug (and leg straps if used).

e. As there are many variations of surcingles and fastenings in current use, each person will need to assess the individual situation and secure the fastenings in whichever order seems most appropriate at the time.

f. If a roller is used to secure the rug, it needs to be firmly buckled to stop the rug from slipping. To prevent undue pressure, there should be plenty of padding between the horse's withers and the roller.

g. Cross-over surcingles incorporated into the rug avoid the pressure problems that rollers can cause and are favoured by many owners. The design is an excellent contribution to the comfort of the horse. They should be adjusted to hang just 3–5 cm (1–2 in) below the horse's belly. This type of rug is usually darted and shaped to fit the contours of the horse's body more closely. This helps to prevent slipping.

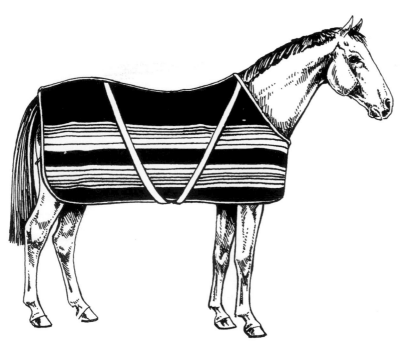

Sheet with cross surcingles

There are many different rugs and rug fastenings on the market. Whatever type of rug and fastening are chosen, it is essential that they are correctly fitted and that the horse is comfortable wearing them. Illustrated here are (above) a rug for stable use, with anti-cast roller and (below) a stable rug with cross surcingles

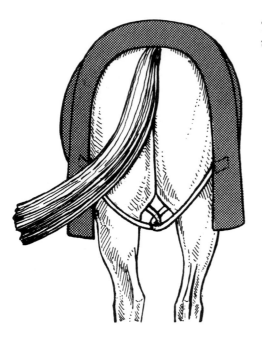

This horse is wearing a New Zealand rug with leg straps linked together

h. As horses are more active in the field, most turnout rugs (New Zealands) have leg straps to help secure them. These should be adjusted to allow freedom of movement and should hang down approximately level with the inner aspect of the second thigh. Fasten one leg strap, then link the other strap through the first one before fastening. The two straps are thus linked together which aids the stability of the rug and prevents rubbing.

i. Blankets are less popular now that fitted under-rugs, made from various materials, are available. If a blanket is used, fold it in half and lay it over the horse, well forward on its neck. Unfold it and slide it back into place. Take each of the front corners in turn and fold them back towards the withers, leaving a triangular section of blanket pointing forward up the horse's neck. Place the rug on top, then fold the triangular section of blanket back over the top of the rug. It may reach far enough back to be secured under the roller but this really depends on how large the blanket is. Fasten the rug in the usual way.

j. When removing rugs, undo leg straps, front straps and rollers or surcingles. Fold any trailing straps over the rug then fold the rug in half by bringing the wither end back towards the tail end. Slide the rug back and off, leaving the horse's hair lying flat.

Further Points

a. All types of rug should be secured with a roller, surcingle, cross surcingles or leg straps. This is sometimes forgotten when sweat or summer sheets are used as they are not always made with surcingles attached.

b. Some turnout rugs are made extra deep at the sides for warmth and protection from the weather.

c. Some rugs may be fitted with a fillet string. This is a piece of cord attached to the two back corners of the rug, which hangs level with the second thigh and fits around the back of the horse's legs under its tail. The fillet string is used to prevent the back of the rug from blowing out and up in breezy conditions. It is particularly useful on light rugs that may be worn outside at shows or when travelling.

d. Rugs should fit snugly around the base of the horse's neck. If the front section hangs low on the chest, the rug will slip back too easily and rub the horse's shoulders. If the length is correct, the rug should reach the top of the horse's tail. If it is much longer or shorter than this, the shaped parts of the rug will not correspond with the shape of the horse.

e. Most rugs will be labelled with washing or cleaning instructions. Those made of washable material may fit in your washing machine, making cleaning easy. (Not all domestic machines are large enough to cope with a large rug.)

• As horses are more active in the field – rolling, kicking, cantering around – most turnout rugs have leg straps which help to keep them secure and stop them slipping off to one side. If rugs do slip, the horse may become caught up and injure itself

Waxed or waterproof rugs will need to be brushed clean and may need rewaxing or reproofing to keep them waterproof. Some companies specialise in rug cleaning and repair. Your saddler will probably know if there is a rug cleaner in your area.

f. How frequently your rugs are washed or cleaned depends entirely upon how much they are worn. A stable rug in constant use will probably need washing every two to four weeks, while a turnout rug may need brushing off regularly and then be cleaned only once a year. Any leather work on your rugs should be oiled and saddle soaped as   frequently as your other tack.

g. When not in use, rugs should be stored on shelves or hangers in a dry atmosphere. Take precautions against moths and vermin; they can easily ruin an expensive rug.

h. Some rugs have woollen linings. These may irritate a horse with sensitive skin, especially if it has been clipped. Other horses may be too warm in a thick, quilted rug, or may fit one particular design of rug better than another. All these factors, and others such as cost, do need to be considered when choosing a rug.

i. The type of sweat rug that resembles a string vest should always be used in conjunction with a second rug. Used on its own, it has no purpose. The idea is for it to trap a layer of air between the horse and the outer rug. This layer of air circulates and helps to dry a wet horse without letting it become chilled.

j. Sweat sheets or coolers come into their own for horses returning hot and sweaty from competition. There are some very good modern designs which draw away moisture from the horse's coat and out to the outer surface of the rug where it evaporates away thus keeping the horse warm while it dries and preventing chills. They are usually fitted with cross surcingles or belly strap and fillet string, which does away with the need for rollers. It must be uncomfortable for the horse to have a firmly fitted roller put around its middle when it has just been relieved of the girth which was holding the saddle on. These modern sheets can also double as summer sheets or travelling rugs, which obviously cuts down on costs.

k. Even on a warm day, it is a good idea to put a cooler/sweat sheet on the horse after a competition. While cooling off and drying, the tired horse can easily begin to feel cold. However, it is also necessary to make sure you don't over-rug and thus distress the horse by making it too warm.

2. Bandages

Bandages are made in different widths, lengths and materials, and for different uses.

Tail Bandage

a. Tail bandages are a little less stretchy than exercise bandages but are made from similar material, approximately 7–8 cm (2³/₄–2 in) wide, with cotton ties.
b. They are used to protect the tail while travelling and to help to improve the horse's appearance by keeping the top of the tail smooth, especially after it has been pulled.

Putting on a tail bandage

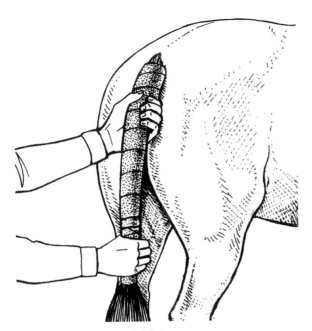

Shape the tail after bandaging

c. A tail bandage should not be left on for more than one hour. As it has to be applied firmly to prevent it from slipping down, it could interfere with circulation if left on too long. This may cause the hair to fall out!

d. Damp the tail hair at the top of the horse's tail before applying the bandage. This aids grip for the first few turns.

e. For even pressure, keep the bandage smooth and overlap each turn evenly, as well as keeping the tension of the tapes, when tied, the same as the bandage.

f. Bandage almost to the end of the dock for a pleasing appearance and a firm base to work around.

g. When travelling, finish the bandage by winding it a few centimetres back up the tail, tie the tapes slightly to one side, and fold the last turn of your bandage down over the tapes to cover them. This helps to prevent them being rubbed undone if the horse leans its tail against the wall in the box. If the bandage is finished and tied too high, the tapes and knot may rub against the horse and cause a sore.

h. Finally, with one hand under the tail, reshape it to follow the contour of the horse's hindquarters so that the horse is not left with its tail sticking out at an uncomfortable angle.

i. To remove the bandage, untie the tapes then slide the whole bandage off in one piece, from the top, down the horse's tail.

Stable/Travelling Bandages

a. Stable/travelling bandages are 10–12 cm (4–4³/₄ in) in width and made from slightly stretchy material which may be wool, cotton or synthetic. They may have cotton ties or Velcro fastenings.

b. They can be used in the stable for warmth, for support after a hard day's competing or to secure a poultice.

c. Used for travelling, they provide support and protection.

d. Fybagee or gamgee is used under these bandages to help to distribute even pressure. When travelling, the Fybagee can be cut long enough to extend above and below the bandage to help to protect the coronet bands, knees and hocks. It is now possible to buy shaped pieces of padding for use under travelling bandages, which make it easier to protect the knees and hocks.

e. Roll the bandage around the horse's leg in the same direction as

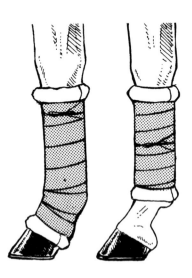

Bandages are made for different uses and in different widths, lengths and materials. The two examples shown here are: (left) *a travelling, or stable, bandage; and* (right) *an exercise bandage*

the overlap of your Fybagee/gamgee. Otherwise the Fybagee/gamgee will be unrolling as you try to bandage.

Further Points

a. Remove all types of leg bandages by passing the bandage quickly from one hand to the other as you unwind it around the horse's leg. The leg will then benefit from a brisk hand massage to restore normal circulation.
b. Leg bandages and tail bandages (apart from Vetwrap) can be hand or machine washed as often as necessary. Tapes should be ironed flat after washing, to prevent them from curling up and making pressure ridges when tied around the horse's leg.
c. Fybagee and gamgee will stand up to gentle hand washing; being stronger, Fybagee will last longer.

3. Further Protective Equipment for Travelling

Make sure your horse is familiar with new equipment before the day of travel. For example, hock boots take time to get used to. Use a minimum of equipment for long journeys, to avoid sores and discomfort. Choose rugs that are suitable for the weather conditions.

Poll Guard

a. If there is not much head room in your box or trailer, and if the horse is tall or inclined to resist while being loaded, this is a useful item.
b. Some guards cover only the poll, while others extend to protect the eyes and forehead.
c. The poll guard attaches to the head collar. When fitting it, check that it will not rub around the ears and that the head collar will not slip back. If a browband is fitted to the head collar, it will prevent both head collar and poll guard from slipping back.

Tail Guard

a. This can be put over a tail bandage for short journeys but should be used on its own for long journeys.
b. This guard protects the very top of the tail. Horses often lean

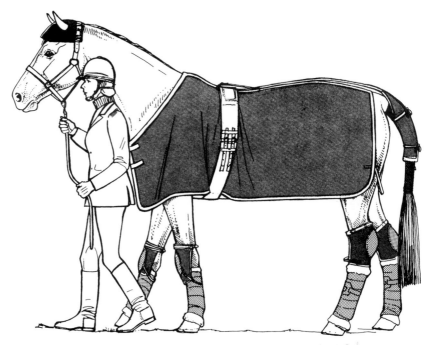

A horse equipped for travelling

against the trailer ramp for support while travelling, causing this area of the tail to be rubbed raw.

c. Tail guards can be made from wool, cotton, leather or synthetic material, and may fasten with buckles, tapes, zips or Velcro, Attach it to the roller at one end, then position the top of the guard just above the top of the tail, wrap it around and fasten.

d. Many modern rugs which do not require rollers to keep them in place are fitted with a small loop of material to which the tail-guard can be attached.

Knee and Hock Boots

a. The knees and hocks are vulnerable when travelling as the horse may lose its balance and stumble or knock its joints against the partitions, etc.

b. These boots must be fitted firmly above the knee
   or hock to prevent them from slipping down.
   For this reason, and for comfort, they
   must be well padded around
   the top strap.

c. The lower strap needs to be
   quite loose to allow the joint
   to flex.

d. Knee boots are also made for
   exercise purposes, to protect the
   knees if the horse stumbles on the
   road. These are called exercise or
   skeleton knee boots. They consist of
   a simple knee cap, often with no
   lower strap and without the extra
   material found on the travelling type.

• Tail guards provide more efficient protection to the tail as, when correctly secured, they do not slip down and can be fitted to protect the very top of the tail, which cannot quite be covered by a tail bandage

Travelling boots

Travelling boots come in many different shapes and sizes and are made from a variety of materials. They are a quick and simple alternative to bandages but do not give the same degree of support to tired legs. Most have Velcro fastenings. Some incorporate knee and hock protection.

Overreach Boots

a. Also called bell boots, these are designed to protect the bulbs of the heels from being trodden on from behind, therefore they are used on the front feet only.

b. They are usually made of rubber. Some fasten with buckles, rubber straps or Velcro and others are made to pull on.

c. They are mainly used for exercise but when used for travelling they help to protect the coronet band as well as the heels.

d. The pull-on variety can be difficult to get on. Soaking them in warm water for a few minutes will help.

Further Points

a. All equipment should be cleaned regularly. Any leather should be soaped and oiled in the usual way. Boots can be brushed or wiped clean depending on the material. Some can go in the washing machine.

Follow-up Work to Confirm Knowledge and Experience

1. It is advisable to practise putting on, checking the fitting and taking off as great a range of equipment as possible. As already mentioned, as so many different designs are now available, confidence will improve if the candidate is familiar with a wide range of designs. Visiting the local saddlery shop is helpful in this.
2. Speed and efficiency are important qualities to develop. A good way to do this is to be involved with horses going to competitions. Having to prepare horses for travelling, which must be ready for a certain deadline, or take care of a horse as it completes its competition, are good ways of improving these qualities.

Helpful Hints and Exam Technique

 Check the available equipment carefully before you select what you are going to use for the task set. In an exam situation it is easy to miss something. Although you will be expected to be quick and efficient, it will be easier for you to do a good job if you have selected the right items to start with.

 In your place of work, practise talking about the equipment you are fitting while you are fitting it. Although you do not have to talk while you work in the exam, there may be something you would like to point out to the examiner who is observing your work. Practising this skill will help you to put over more information as you go along. However, you should remember that the ability to perform the practical skill is the most important part of the practical sections, rather than an ability to talk about it.

9 Clipping, Trimming, Plaiting and Finishing Touches

Your horse's fitness and general appearance will benefit from the attention and care you show it. Along with regular grooming, there are a number of finishing touches which will help towards this goal.

1. Reasons for Clipping

a. By removing all or part of a thick winter coat, we can enable a horse to continue to work without the distress caused by becoming hot and sweaty. This also enables us to keep the horse fit for work.
b. The horse will cool and dry off quickly after work. This helps to prevent chills and is labour saving.
c. It is easier to keep a clipped horse clean and to spot the first signs of heat and swelling, etc. This, in turn, can help to prevent disease.
d. Clipping can improve the horse's appearance.

2. Preparing the Horse for Clipping

a. Clipper blades will not run smoothly through a dirty coat. The horse should preferably be stabled and groomed thoroughly for several days before clipping. Wearing a light rug will also help to keep the coat clean.
b. If the horse is not familiar with the clippers, try to stand it next to a well-behaved horse while that horse is being clipped. This will help the first horse to get used to the noise and it will absorb the feeling from the other horse that this is not a frightening experience.

c. Familiarise the horse with the clipping machine by resting it (switched off) against its coat. Move the clippers over the horse's body, giving the horse a chance to see the machine and electric cable.

d. When the horse is relaxed with the machine switched off, stand away from it and turn the clippers on. Reassure the horse, then approach and rest the clippers against its shoulder without actually clipping. Again move the clippers over the coat to let the horse feel the vibration.

e. It may be necessary to introduce the clippers over a period of several days. Once the horse is confident, you will be able to begin clipping.

f. Plait the horse's mane and bandage the tail to keep them out of the way.

g. Have a blanket ready to place over the newly clipped areas in order to keep the horse warm.

h. The horse's coat must be completely dry.

i. Outline the type of clip to be followed by drawing on the horse's coat with chalk or saddle soap. Check that the saddle patch, blanket, etc., are drawn the same size and depth on each side.

j. For a hunter clip, draw around the horse's usual saddle to make a saddle patch outline. If the horse wears both dressage and jumping saddles, combine the two by following the straight-cut front of the dressage saddle and the shorter flap length of the jumping saddle.

3. Preparation and Choice of the Clipping Area

a. To see clearly what and where you are clipping, plenty of daylight is needed. At the same time, you need to be prepared for poor weather, so good electric lighting is also required.

b. An area that is sheltered from wind and rain is essential. The horse should not be subjected to draughts and the machinery must be kept dry.

c. The flooring must be non-slip. A purpose-built area with rubber matting on the floor is ideal. This provides a non-slip surface that can be cleaned easily and will provide some degree of insulation in the case of an electrical fault. Alternatively, a thin layer of straw can be laid on the stable floor.

d. A power point is needed, with a circuit breaker for safety.

e. It is helpful to have a ceiling hook for the electric cable to run through. This will keep the cable off the floor where it may otherwise be stepped on by the horse.

4. The Clipping Machine and its Care

a. Check that the clippers are in good working order. They should be serviced by an expert after each season's use.

b. Make sure the cable is intact, with no splits in the outer cover and no loose connections at either plug or machine end.

c. Clippers should be fitted with a wrist strap for safety. Put your hand through the strap, then hold the clippers. If the horse moves suddenly and you lose your grip, the clippers should end up swinging from your wrist rather than crashing to the ground.

d. The whole machine must be very clean. Check that the air vents are not clogged with hair.

e. The blades must be very sharp and will need to be resharpened after, approximately, one full clip or two blanket clips. Select coarse blades for long thick coats and finer blades for short fine coats.

f. Secure the blades and adjust the tension according to the manufacturer's instructions. (Approximate guide for tension: turn the tension screw until you feel some resistance, then make one and a half more turns.) If the tension is too tight, the machine will quickly overheat; if too loose, the blades will not clip.

g. The machine needs to be well oiled using clipper oil only. Thicker oils will reduce the efficiency of the machine and eventually stop it from working. Apply oil to the blades.

h. Plug in and switch on. Allow the machine to run for a few moments while the oil works in. The clippers are now ready for use.

i. During clipping, test the flat blade against the back of your hand every 15 minutes or so. If it is getting hot, it will scorch the horse, so then you need to stop and allow the blades to cool. A variety of cooling fluids are available for spraying on to the blades.

Preparing to clip the horse: (opposite page, top) *cleaning the clippers;* (opposite page, bottom) *adjusting the tension screw; and* (this page) *oiling the clippers*

j. While the blades are cooling, remove them from the clippers and clean away all the loose hair. You will need a soft brush and a cloth with which to keep the air vents, blades and head of the clippers clean.

k. During a full clip, you will probably stop approximately four to six times to cool the blades, clean the machine and re-oil it.

l. After clipping, remove and clean the blades. Store them in oiled cloth or paper to prevent rusting. Thoroughly clean the machine and wrap the head in oiled cloth. Store in a dry place.

5. Different Types of Clip

a. Full clip – All of the coat is removed. A good clip to improve the appearance of thick-coated horses. Used for fit, stabled horses in hard work.

b. Hunter clip – The legs and saddle patch are left on, the rest of the

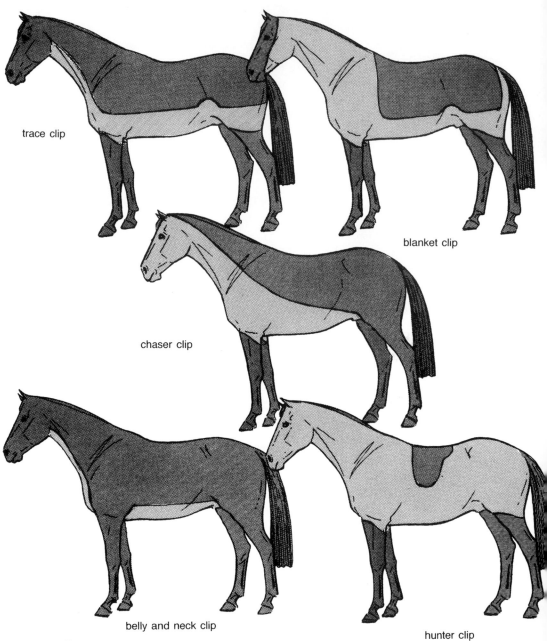

trace clip

blanket clip

chaser clip

belly and neck clip

hunter clip

Different types of clip

coat is removed. Used for hunters as the leg hair protects the horse from thorns, etc., in undergrowth, while the saddle patch protects the back from the saddle and a rider who may stay mounted for several hours. Suitable for all stabled, fit horses in hard work.

c. Blanket clip – The hair is left on the legs and in a blanket shape over the horse's back. Suitable for stabled horses that feel the cold, suffer from azoturia or are in medium work.

d. Chaser clip – The hair is removed from beneath a sloping line that runs from the stifle up to the poll. The hair is left on the legs. This is a variation of the blanket clip, used for the same reasons. It is also useful if the horse is reluctant to be clipped around the hind legs.

e. Trace clip – The hair is removed below a horizontal line running from mid-thigh to the point of the shoulder, including a strip up the underside of the horse's neck. The hair is left on the legs. This is suitable for working horses kept at grass in a New Zealand rug.

Blanket clip

f. Belly and neck clip – This clip has various names and involves removing a small amount of hair from under the belly and the underside of the neck. It is suitable for field-kept ponies that may not be rugged up but are inclined to sweat when worked.

g. There are many variations on the above clips. The height of blanket, chaser and trace clips may vary. Owners may alter the style in order to improve the horse's appearance. For example, a high leg line will make the legs look longer.

h. The face hair may be left on with any clip if the horse is reluctant to have its head clipped. Alternatively, half the face hair can be removed, by following the vertical line made by the cheekpiece of the bridle.

6. How to Clip

a. The hair removed will stick to your clothes, so wear overalls and a head scarf or hat. You may even like to wear a face mask. It is also advisable to wear rubber-soled footwear in case of an electrical fault.

b. The shoulder is usually the best place to start. It is a smooth, easily accessible area, not ticklish and a safe distance from the

The shoulder is usually the best place to start clipping

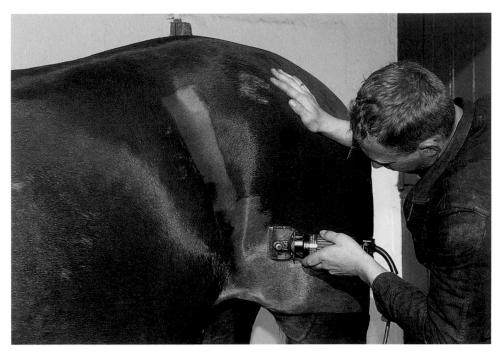

Clipping the horse

hind legs. Providing the horse relaxes after the first few strokes, you can then progress to any part of the body.

c. The difficult parts of the process are making smooth, straight, even lines and obtaining a neat finish around areas like the elbows and head. If the horse is relaxed, tackle these areas first, while you and the horse are at your most patient.

d. Press the clippers flat against the horse's skin and run them into the coat against the lie of the hair. By making long, smooth strokes, you will gain a smoother finish.

e. Each time the lie of the hair changes, for example when you meet a whorl, you will need to change the direction of the clippers so that you continue to clip against the lie of the hair.

f. In order not to pinch the horse, you will need to use your spare hand to smooth the horse's skin, especially in areas like the neck and behind the elbow where the skin wrinkles easily.

g. If removing the hair from the quarters, make a neat finish at the top of the tail by forming a small triangle.

h. When clipping the neck, take care not to remove any of the mane as this will result in unsightly tufts as it grows out.

i. It is better not to give a horse a hay net. Each time it pulls hay, the movement will make it difficult for you to keep the clippers steady.

j. It is useful to have an assistant to hold up each of the front legs in turn as you clip around the elbows. It may also be necessary to hold up a leg to encourage the horse to stay still while a ticklish area is clipped.

k. You will probably need a stool to stand on in order to reach some areas.

l. Don't forget to check the heat of the blades frequently. Keep brushing them clean and apply more oil or cooling spray at regular intervals.

m. Start clipping early in the day. This will allow you plenty of daylight hours if the horse proves difficult. You need to complete the clip within one day to avoid it looking patchy.

7. Further Points

a. Most horses have their first clip in September/October when the winter coat is well through. However, if your horse is just starting a fitness programme at this time of year, leave the coat on for warmth until you have completed the walking stage. You may need to reclip two or three times during the winter. Plan the last clip for January/February. By the time this clip has grown out, the winter coat will be ready to moult.

b. An experienced clipper will complete a full or hunter clip in 45–60 minutes, providing the horse is well behaved. Difficult horses can take all day to complete.

c. Many horses behave well until it comes to clipping their heads. It is probably the noise that worries them or it may be the vibration. Some will stand quietly if twitched. Alternatively, they may tolerate the type of clippers used for dogs. These are small and tend to purr, which is less frightening. If a horse is very frightened of clipping in general, you can arrange for your vet to sedate the horse.

d. Immediately after clipping, rub down the clipped areas with a hot damp towel. This will open the pores and lift off grease and loose hair.

8. Methods of Restraint

a. If a horse is being difficult to restrain (not just for clipping), the simplest way of keeping it under control is to put on a bridle. This may give you sufficient control.
b. A Chifney bit could be put on for further control. This type of bit seems to help to prevent a horse from rearing and is also known as an anti-rearing bit.
c. A neck twitch can be of help. This entails pinching a piece of loose skin and holding firmly. It can be an effective way of distracting a horse long enough to get it to stand still while the job is done.
d. If the horse is still too difficult to manage, a twitch can be applied to the top lip. Care must be taken not to leave the twitch on for more than a minute or two at a time, otherwise the circulation will be cut off and permanent damage done, so this type of twitch is not suitable for a long job. A twitch with a piece of cord on the end or the humane twitch, which is made of metal, can be used. The theory behind this type of twitching is that it causes the horse to release endorphins into its system. These are natural pain-relieving substances and are supposed to have a calming effect on the horse. However, some horses fight against being twitched, which can be dangerous.
e. Sometimes, just holding up a leg will be enough to restrain a horse. If examining the near hind, hold up the near fore as the horse will find it difficult to stand on two legs on the same side of its body, but can balance quite well on a diagonal pair.
f. The horse can be sedated for a procedure like clipping if it is particularly frightened of being clipped. By sedating the horse you may help it to become relaxed and accept the clipping process.
g. Hobbles can be used to restrain a horse from kicking. This is sometimes done to mares when being covered to prevent them from injuring the stallion.
h. It is *not* a good idea to hold a horse's ear or tongue to restrain it.

If the horse pulls away violently, the tongue or ear can literally be ripped away!

i. Good use of your facilities is important when restraining a horse. For example, check that there is plenty of head room as a horse will panic even more if it throws its head up and hits it on the ceiling. Move the horse over into a corner of its box to make use of the wall to help to keep the horse still.

9. Trimming

a. Use blunt, curved-ended scissors for trimming to help to prevent injury to the horse.

b. Many horses have long tufts of hair sprouting from their ears. The hair inside the ears is needed to protect the inner ear from entry by foreign particles but the longer tufts that stick out can be trimmed. Gently close the edges of the ears together, then trim away the long hair that is still protruding, cutting it level with the edges of the ear.

c. Make a path for the bridle. Do this by cutting away a section of mane, approximately 3 cm (1½ in), just behind the ears where the bridle headpiece will sit. Use a comb to make a neat parting between mane and forelock prior to cutting.

d. Some horses grow long hair under the lower jaw, like a beard. This can be trimmed close to the jaw bone.

e. Some owners prefer to trim away the long whiskers that grow around the horse's muzzle area. But these whiskers are part of the horse's sensory equipment and I prefer to leave them untrimmed.

f. About 8–10 cm (3–4 in) of mane over the withers may be trimmed away if it tends to get tangled under the saddle and numnah.

g. Removing the feathers at the back of the horse's legs will improve its appearance and make it easier to keep the lower limbs clean. Using a comb, comb the hair upwards, then trim the hair away level with the comb. This leaves a smooth finish.

h. To trim the end of the tail, first check the required length by asking an assistant to place a hand under the dock, lifting the tail to simulate the position in which the horse will carry it when

moving. Then trim the bottom of the tail parallel to the ground so that it hangs approximately 12 cm (4³/₄ in) below the point of the hock. This is known as a banged tail.

i. Some owners prefer not to trim any areas, particularly if they have a native pony, as these ponies are always shown in their natural state.

10. Pulling Manes and Tails

Manes

a. Manes are pulled to make them neat, tidy, easy to manage and short and thin enough to plait.

b. The hair will come out more easily when the horse is warm and the pores are open.

c. If the horse has a very long and thick mane, the hair should be removed over a period of several days, otherwise the horse will become sore and irritable.

Pulling the horse's mane

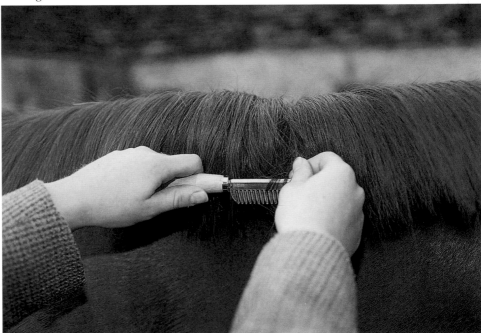

d. Comb the mane to remove tangles. Hold a few of the long hairs between thumb and finger, while pushing back the shorter hairs with the comb. Wrap the long hairs around the comb, then give the comb a quick tug. The long hairs should come out by the roots.

e. Work gradually up and down the mane, removing the long hairs and trying to keep the mane level.

f. The forelock is pulled in the same way.

Tails

a. Tails are pulled to give the top a neat appearance, which also helps to show off the hindquarters to their best advantage.

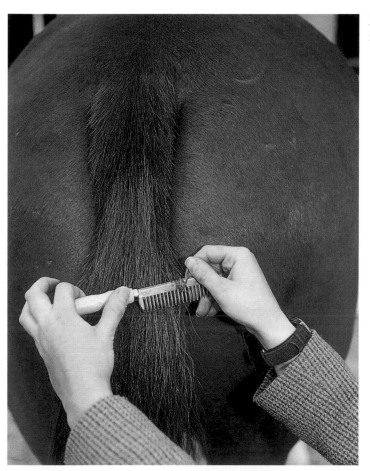

Pulling the horse's tail

b. If the horse has not had its tail pulled before, it may kick if it finds the process uncomfortable. Stand the horse with its hindquarters backed up to its stable door, while you stand on the other side for protection.

c. Remove the hairs gradually over a period of days.

d. Use comb and fingers to remove a few hairs at a time (in the same way as pulling the mane) from either side of the dock.

e. Work from the top, approximately 18–20 cm (7–7^1/$_4$ in) down each side.

f. Finish by putting on a tail bandage for a short period of time. This will encourage the hairs to lie flat.

11. Plaiting

The mane

a. A short, well-pulled mane will make plaiting easier.

b. You will need needle, thread and scissors or plaiting bands, a stool to stand on, water and water brush to damp the mane, and a comb.

c. Plaiting bands and thread can be obtained in different colours to suit your horse.

d. Never plait with needle and thread while the horse is standing on bedding. If you drop the needle it will be lost, which will necessitate the removal of the whole bed.

e. Through trial and error, you will discover how much mane to take for each plait. As a rough guide, use the width of your mane comb to measure each section.

f. Using plaiting bands, divide the mane into even-sized bunches. The number of plaits will depend upon the length of the horse's neck, the size of each plait and the thickness of the mane.

g. Push the comb into the mane to keep the loose hair out of the way.

h. Start at the poll and work back towards the withers. Damp the first section of mane, then divide it into three even sections and plait to the end. Keep the plait tight.

i. Secure the end of the plait with a plaiting band, or with thread. Use the thread doubled with a knot in the end.

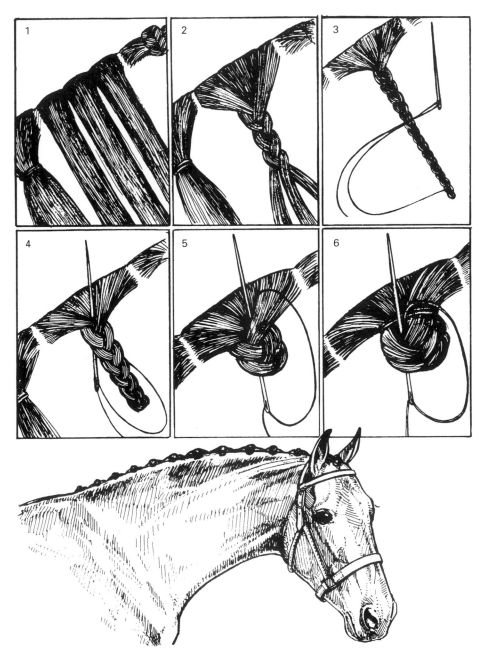

Six steps to plaiting the mane

j.   If using bands, roll up the plait and secure it as tightly as possible with a second band.

k.   If using thread, fold the plait in half, by taking the bottom up to the top, and stitch this together. Fold again and then once more (depending on the length of the plait), securing the fold with a stitch each time.

l.   Finish off by winding the thread once or twice around the base of the plait, then draw the thread through the whole plait and cut the thread off.

m.   Do not trim off any protruding wisps of hair. This will ruin the mane, leaving it uneven and spiky when not plaited.

n.   It is customary to have an uneven number of plaits in the mane plus one forelock plait.

The Tail

a.   Brush and comb the tail, then thoroughly damp the hair to be plaited.

b.   Take a small section of hair from the top at either side and a small section from the middle, giving you three sections to begin plaiting with.

c.   Progress down the dock, taking small sections of hair from either side and adding them into your plait.

d.   Keep the plait very tight.

e.   When you reach the end of the dock, make one long plait from the remaining lengths of hair.

f.   Secure the end of the plait with thread or a plaiting band. Double it up to make a loop, securing it with thread or plaiting bands at the end of the main dock plait.

12. Finishing Touches

a.   Quarter markings can be applied by placing a stencil on the coat then body brushing the hair at right angles to its normal direction of growth. When the stencil is removed, an attractive pattern is left on the coat. This can also be done without a stencil. You can practise making different patterns with a body brush or comb.

b.   To darken black skin around the eyes and muzzle and add an

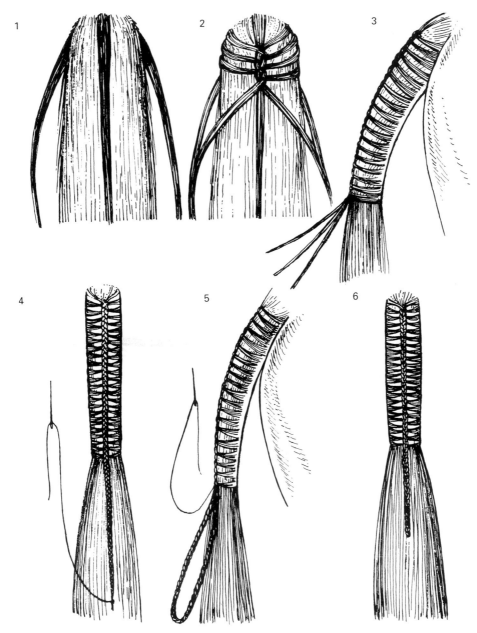

Six steps to plaiting the tail

attractive gloss, a thin layer of baby oil can be applied. Tip a small drop into the palm of your hand. Rub your hands together and then wipe over the horse's muzzle and eyes.

c. Rub chalk into white legs. This is especially effective if the horse has thickly feathered legs.

d. Hoof oil gives a shine to the wall of the foot.

- Use curved, blunt-ended scissors for trimming to help to prevent injury to the horse. But do make sure they are sharp enough to cut hair cleanly; blunt scissors will pull the hair and cause the horse to become fractious

Follow-up Work to Confirm Knowledge and Experience

1. It is necessary to have completed at least one clip in order to experience and understand all aspects of the process really well. Clipping several horses will give more experience of how different horses react and how their coats can be different to clip.

2. Pulling and plaiting manes and tails of several different horses gives experience in handling different types of mane and different reactions from the horses. Experience in plaiting a horse ready for a competition is a good way of improving speed and efficiency.

Helpful Hints and Exam Technique

 When plaiting a mane in an examination situation, you may only be required to put in one or two plaits but you need to approach the task as if you were going to tackle the whole mane. Start at the poll, not in the middle of the mane.

 When handling the clippers, show that you are aware that they are an expensive and easily damaged item of equipment. If they are of a design that you have not seen before, say so, and show that you can work out how to put on the blades and check the equipment using your experience of other designs of clippers. You are not expected to have experience of every different type but if you really have worked with clippers you should be able to cope with any different design.

10 Travelling

Travelling the horse involves more than the journey itself. There is a need to observe a number of stages, each of equal importance, to ensure the safety and comfort of the horse at all times and to prevent the horse arriving at its destination in a distressed state.

1. Preparation

a. Check that the vehicles are roadworthy; for example, road tax, brakes, oil, water, tyres, lights, connections, etc.
b. Park the vehicle in a safe location for loading; for example, an enclosed area from which the horse cannot escape. Use a quiet area with as few distractions as possible. An inexperienced horse may distrust the loading process and attempt to break loose. Distractions may cause the horse to back out of the box or to refuse to go in at all.
c. The ramp must rest firmly and not rock on uneven ground.
d. Both ramp and internal flooring must be non-slip. Rubber matting is ideal. This can be lifted out and washed clean periodically. At the same time, check that the floor underneath is sound and not showing any signs of rotting. Alternatively, straw will provide a good surface, but must be cleaned out frequently.
e. The inside of the box must be free of any protrusions that might cause an injury if leant against or knocked into.
f. Partitions, breast bars and doors must be completely secure.
g. Check that there is string on the tie up rings.
h. Remove loose items, such as buckets, which might move or rattle and become entangled with or frighten the horse.
i. If the horse is likely to be difficult, park the box alongside a wall or hedge. This will help to guide the horse up the ramp. It is also helpful to park the box with its rear towards a slope or bank, if available. When the ramp is let down, it will rest on the slope,

127

making it level or nearly so. With less of a slope, the horse will walk in with more confidence.

j. Horses may feel claustrophobic and/or cautious about entering an enclosed box. To help, open any top front doors of a trailer, push partitions to one side and make the compartment as airy and light as possible. With a front-unload trailer, keep the front ramp closed or the horse may try to rush in and go straight out of the front opening.

2. Loading

a. The horse, clothed for travelling, should be led out with a bridle over the top of its head collar and rope. A bridle gives you more control when leading. Once in the box, the bridle can be slipped off, leaving the head collar and lead rope to tie the horse up with.

b. The leader must wear gloves, hard hat and strong footwear for protection. It may also be helpful to carry a stick. A quick tap may be all it takes to encourage a hesitant horse.

c. The horse should be led at a purposeful walk straight towards the ramp.

d. An assistant must be available to put up the ramp and also to help if the horse is reluctant to go in. Take care never to stand directly behind a ramp, as it may fall on you if the horse rushes backwards. Two assistants are needed for safe opening and closing of heavy ramps.

e. Always keep looking straight ahead. Never look back towards the horse, even if it stops. You will only discourage forward activity.

f. Once in, hold the horse while the breaching strap is fastened and the ramp or partition is locked in place. The horse is now secure and can be tied up with a quick release knot.

g. Take care not to give the horse

• The horse, clothed for travelling, should be lead out with a bridle over the top of its head collar and rope. This gives the handler full control. Then, once in the box or trailer, the bridle can be removed and the horse tied up with head collar and rope

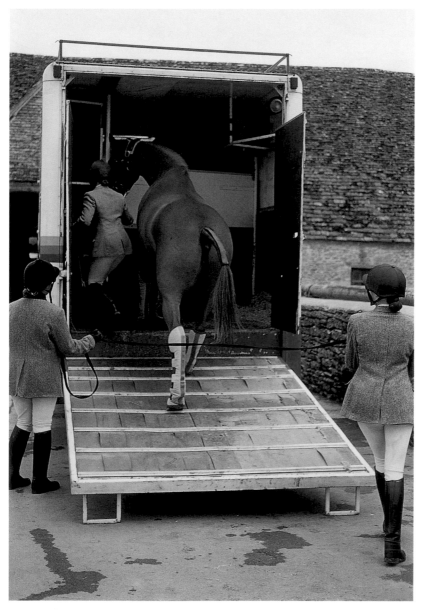

Loading the horse. Note the two assistants use the lunge line to encourage the horse to enter the box

too much rope when tied up. It should not be able to fight with the horse next door, get its head caught under the front of the partition or attempt to turn round.

h. For horses which chew their ropes, have a length of chain tied to the tie up string and clip this to the head collar once the horse is loaded. The lead rope can then be removed.

3. The Difficult Loader

If the horse refuses to enter the box, there are several ways to encourage it. Different tactics work with different horses. Remember to build up the horse's confidence and do not scare it. All handlers should wear protective clothing.

a. An assistant can stand inside the box and offer a small bucket of feed. Allow the horse a mouthful of feed each time it progresses a few steps.

b. Two assistants can hold a lunge line or soft rope around the horse's hindquarters, just above its hocks. Pressure is applied as the assistants walk forward on either side of the horse. This encourages the horse to walk forward. Take great care not to let the horse become entangled in the line.

c. Some horses suddenly gain confidence if each of their feet is picked up in turn and placed a little further up the ramp. In effect, you are moving the horse's legs for it.

d. More experienced but stubborn characters will often respond to a quick tap with a whip on their hindquarters or a quick prod with the brush end of a yard broom.

e. Load a well-behaved and experienced horse into the box first. This may give confidence to the other horse and encourage it to go in.

f. Whatever happens, it is vital that the leader should keep the horse straight. If the horse understands that it cannot escape around the side of the box, it will eventually go forward.

g. Reward the horse with feed once it is inside and secure.

h. Because of the enclosed space in which you are working, and the nature of the frightened horse,

- If the journey is comfortable, the horse will gain confidence and become a willing traveller. Calm handlers make for calm horses

If a horse refuses to load, there are several ways to encourage it; placing a foreleg on the ramp (above) may give the horse confidence and (left) a lunge line behind the horse may help to encourage it forward

loading horses into boxes or trailers is potentially dangerous and every care and precaution should be taken.

4. Unloading

a. Untie the horse before the breaching strap is undone, the ramp let down or the partition opened.
b. If the horse is likely to be difficult, slip on a bridle for greater control.
c. With a box or trailer designed for the horse to walk out forwards, simply encourage it to walk slowly. Allow it to stop and take in its surroundings if it wants to. Keep it straight to prevent it from hitting its hips on the side of the box or slipping off the edge of the ramp.
d. If you are using a rear-unload trailer, the horse's main problem is not being able to see what it is backing out on to. Assistants should stand on each side of the ramp and place a hand on the horse's hindquarters to guide it straight and reassure it.
e. The horse may try to turn around which will make it particularly inclined to come out crooked. Once it can see where it is, allow it to look around and take everything in.

5. The Journey

a. If the horse has a smooth and comfortable journey, it will gain confidence and become a willing traveller, walking confidently in and out of the box when required.
b. Stopping and starting at crossings and driving round bends require adjustments in the horse's balance, therefore the driver must make sure there are very gradual changes in speed and direction to prevent injury to the horse or loss of confidence.
c. Be aware that low branches scraping against the roof of the box, or any other unexplained noises, will frighten the horse. Try to avoid this when possible.
d. Young horses should gain confidence from travelling with a companion.
e. It is important to assess the weather conditions along with the type of box before deciding what clothing to put on the horse.

When travelling, the horse can generate a considerable amount of heat. If there are several horses in the box and the box is quite enclosed, each horse can become quite hot, especially if the rugs worn are too thick. This can cause the horse to become distressed.

Follow-up Work to Confirm Knowledge and Experience

1. It is a good idea to watch and then assist with loading and unloading horses in order to gain experience gradually. Then practise loading and unloading well-behaved horses. In time, working with a variety of horses, you are bound to come across various horses which are problematical to load and unload. Through these horses you will gain experience and expertise in handling such situations.
2. Try to gain experience with a variety of horseboxes and trailers. Each different type has ramps, fastenings, partitions, fittings and floorings that differ from each other.

11 The Lower Limb and Shoeing

Understanding some of the farrier's work and the structure of the lower limb and foot will help the horse owner to keep the horse's feet in good condition.

1. The Structure of the Lower Limb and Foot

a. The foot is designed to support the horse, reduce concussion, resist wear and provide grip.
b. Because we demand more from the horse than nature intended, the foot often needs protection to prevent it from wearing down more quickly than it can regrow. By means of shoeing, the foot is protected and extra grip is provided.
c. Shoeing can also be used to correct faults and heal ailments and injuries.

The External Structure of the Foot

a. The outer wall of the hoof is hard and insensitive. Divided into toe, quarters and heels, it doesn't quite form a circle because it turns inwards at the heels to form the bars. This allows for expansion and provides extra strength at the heels. The wall is made of horn which contains many tubules that grow down from the top to the bottom of the wall.
b. The coronet band forms the junction between the lower limb and the wall.
c. From just above the coronet grows the periople. This is a thin layer of skin that grows down over the wall and controls evaporation of moisture from the horn.
d. Most of the ground surface of the foot consists of the sole which is concave to the ground.

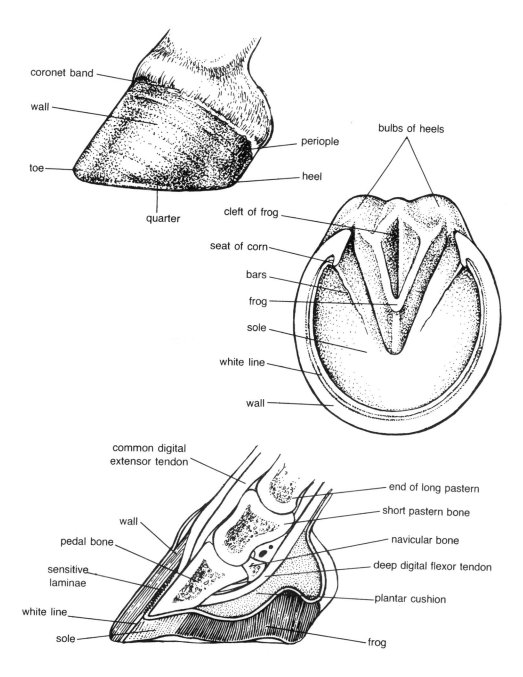

The structure of the foot

e. The white line can be seen between the edge of the sole and the wall. This is the visible part of the horny laminae.

f. The area of sole between the wall and the bars is called the seat of corn.

g. The rest of the ground surface is occupied by the frog. This is wedge-shaped, formed from soft, elastic horn and has a central cleft. It aids grip and helps to absorb concussion.

h. At the rear of the hoof are the bulbs of the heels.

The Internal Structure of the Foot

a. The inner aspect of the wall is lined with the horny laminae, then the sensitive laminae which interlock with the pedal bone and help to support it within the foot.

b. Above the sole is the sensitive sole.

c. The bones within the foot consist of the pedal bone, the navicular bone and part of the short pastern bone.

d. The deep flexor tendon of the lower limb passes into the foot, under the navicular bone and attaches to the pedal bone. The common digital extensor tendon of the lower limb passes into the foot, over the short pastern bone and attaches to the pedal bone.

e. Above the frog is the plantar cushion.

f. These sensitive, internal structures are supplied with blood through many capillaries. They also help the horse to feel and sense what it is walking on.

g. Around the sides of the foot are the lateral cartilages which merge with the bulbs of the heels.

h. being elastic, the frog, bars, plantar cushion and lateral cartilages all help to absorb concussion and disperse it upwards and outwards.

2. The Shoeing Process and the Farrier's Tools

To train as a farrier is a long and expensive process. As a result, there is a shortage of good, reliable farriers. It will be to your advantage to help your farrier to do a good job.

a. Let your farrier know in advance if your horse requires any

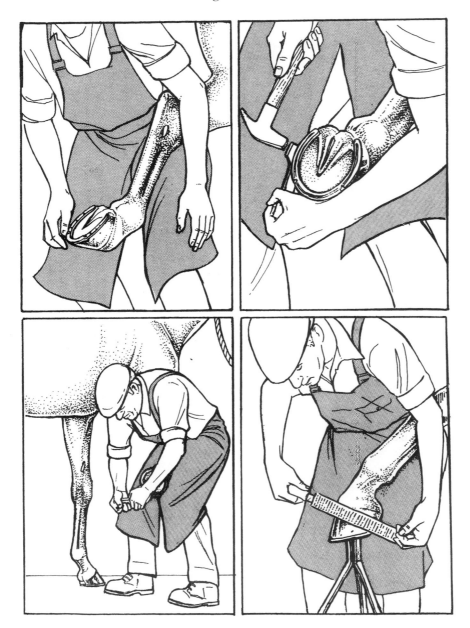

Holding the foot: (top) *the farrier supports the horse's hind foot on his legs, leaving his hands free to use tools; and* (bottom) *the horse's front foot is supported between the farrier's legs or on a tripod, again leaving the farrier's hands free*

*A farrier
at work*

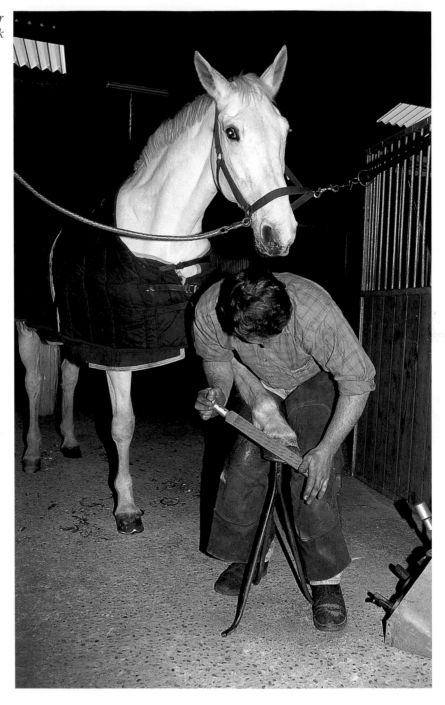

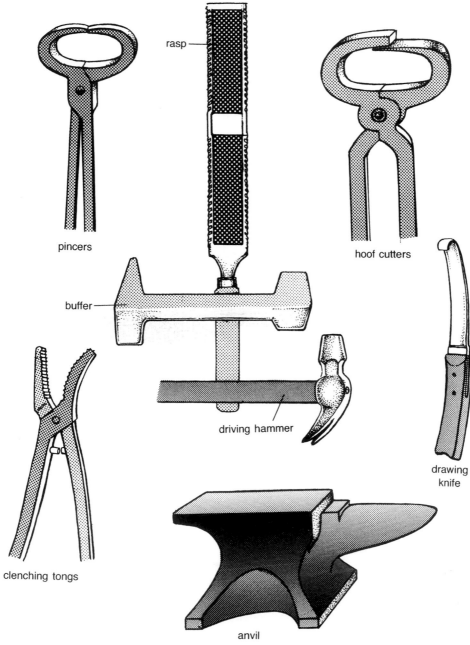

rasp

pincers

hoof cutters

buffer

driving hammer

drawing
knife

clenching tongs

anvil

Shoeing tools

special type of shoes, or if it is a youngster being shod for the first time.

b. Horses being shod for the first time should be used to having their feet picked out and be familiar with having the wall and sole of the foot tapped, to prepare them for the nailing-on process.

c. You should always present horses for shoeing with clean, dry feet and legs.

d. Provide the farrier with a well-lit area and dry, hard standing, if possible undercover.

e. The first time the farrier shoes your horse, he or she should find out about its way of going and, assuming the horse is already shod, should also look at the wear of its shoes and the growth of its feet. With your help, the farrier will then be able to determine whether the horse has any problems, such as overreaching, stumbling, dragging its toes, etc. With problems such as these, the farrier may choose a different type of shoe.

f. If the farrier is hot shoeing, he or she will have brought a mobile forge in which to heat shoes. Using fire tongs, the farrier will place the selected shoes in the forge to heat them ready for use.

g. Next, the farrier will remove the old shoes. The buffer, driving hammer and pincers will be used in this process. The flat end of the buffer is placed under the clench. When hit with the hammer the buffer eases under the clench to lever it up. When all the clenches have been "knocked up", the pincers are used to lever off the shoe, working from the heel towards the toe. Care is taken not to break off any chunks of horn. A front foot may be supported between the farrier's knees, to leave the

• The foot supports the horse's weight and absorbs concussion as it travels across the ground. The shoe helps to resist wear and provides grip. Problems with the feet and poor choice of shoes are sometimes the cause of ailments and injuries in other parts of the horse's body

hands free to hold and use the tools. The farrier's apron provides protection and comfort at this stage. A hind foot will not be held in this way, as the horse could kick out and knock the farrier over!

h. Depending on how much growth of foot there is, the hoof cutters, drawing knife and toeing knife will now be used to remove excess growth of horn.

i. The rasp will then be used to level off the surface to which the shoe will be applied. The rasp or the drawing knife is used to make a notch for the toe clip. This process of preparing the foot for the shoe is called "dressing" the foot.

j. One of the hot shoes will now be removed from the forge with the fire tongs. It will be placed on the anvil and the pritchel will be knocked into one of the nail holes to enable the farrier to carry the hot shoe to the horse.

k. Using the pritchel, the farrier will put the hot shoe firmly into place on the foot so that it burns into the insensitive horn. This process allows the farrier to see if the foot preparation has been done correctly and if the shoe has been shaped to fit as perfectly as possible.

l. The farrier will make adjustments, where necessary, by taking the shoe back to the anvil. While holding the shoe with the shoe tongs, the farrier will hammer it into shape with the turning hammer, often returning it to the forge to be reheated. He or she may also further improve the shape and levelness of the foot with the rasp.

m. Once the farrier is completely happy with the fit of the shoe, he or she will cool the shoe in a bucket of water and prepare to nail it on.

n. In order to make sure that the shoe is nailed evenly in place, the farrier will hammer in the nails by alternating from side to side, usually starting at the toe. Once the nail is driven in, the claw end of the driving hammer is used to twist off the sharp end of the nail.

o. The blunt end of the nails, left after the sharp points have been twisted off, will now be knocked down to form the clenches. The farrier will place the horse's foot on the tripod and use the rasp to make a "bed" in the wall of the foot to knock the clenches into.

The clenching tongs will be used to pull the clenches down tightly. The farrier may also hammer down the clenches.

p. The whole process will be finished off with the rasp, which will be used to smooth off any ragged bits of horn that may be overlapping the shoe. A well-shod foot should appear flush with the shoe all the way round and the clenches should be fairly level, approximately a third of the way up the wall. At the toe the wall of the foot should slope at an angle of approximately 45 degrees in the front feet and 50 degrees in the hind feet.

3. Parts of the Shoe

a. Toe clip/quarter clips – These help to keep the shoe in place on the horse's foot and prevent it from slipping backwards or sideways.

b. The fuller – This is the groove in which the nail heads sit. This helps to prevent the nail heads from wearing away too quickly and also aids grip.

c. The ground-bearing/foot-bearing surfaces.

d. Pencilled heels – Help to prevent the heels of the shoe from being trodden on from behind and therefore help to prevent the shoe being pulled off.

e. The nail holes – Usually four on the outside branch of the shoe and three on the inside branch. The farrier will generally use only as many nails as are necessary to keep the shoe in place. Smaller ponies will have fewer nails.

f. Concave slope – This slope makes the shoe concave to the ground, thereby helping to prevent the shoe from being sucked off in heavy going.

4. Recognising the Need for Reshoeing

Most horses need reshoeing every four to six weeks. This will depend upon how much road/hard ground work the horse does, how quickly the hoof grows and whether the shoe becomes twisted, loose, lost, etc.

a. Part or all of the shoe has worn thin, resulting in less grip. This can be dangerous, especially when riding on the road.

Horse's hoof in need of reshoeing; there is evidence of risen clenches, broken hoof and worn shoe

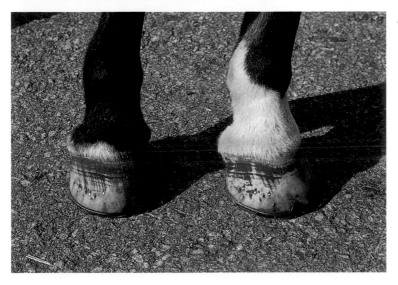

A well-shod hoof

A hoof badly in need of re-shoeing. It is very overgrown, with risen clenches and a worn shoe

b. A loose shoe may twist off at any time. The cast shoe may then be trodden on by the horse, causing a nail to puncture its sole.

c. Risen clenches – The shoe will soon be loose and a risen clench can cause damage if the horse brushes.

d. Long feet – If the foot looks long at the toe, pick it up and examine the heel area. Excess growth will have moved the shoe forward, causing the foot to grow over the shoe at the heels. This

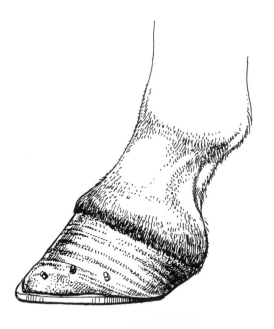

Long foot, with risen clenches, in need of reshoeing

can push the heels of the shoe into the seat of corn, resulting in bruising and lameness.

e. The horse may have cast a shoe. In this case check that all the nails have been removed from the wall.

f. Twisted shoe – Due to the shoe being trodden on by another horse, or by the horse treading on a front shoe with a hind foot, it may be twisted. This could lead to lameness.

g. Cracked and broken feet – Horses with brittle feet may lose chunks of horn. This is likely to loosen the shoe.

5. Further Points on Shoeing

a. If a horse's shoes are hardly worn, the farrier may reshoe the horse with the same set of shoes. This process is called a "remove".

b. Cold shoeing takes place if the farrier does not have a mobile forge. It does not quite equal the close, precise fit achieved by hot shoeing. When the horse is hot shod, the farrier can make more precise alterations to the shoes and therefore create a better fit.

c. If you live near to the farrier's work base, you may hack your horse to him or her rather than have the farrier travelling to you.

d. It takes a day or two for the horn of the horse's hoof to bed down around the newly driven nails. During this period the shoe is less secure, therefore it is unwise to ride your horse at faster paces or through mud for the first day or two; if you do, you may find that the new shoes are lost.

- The horse should always be presented for shoeing with feet and legs clean and dry. This will enable the farrier to carry out shoeing without interference from mud and wet

e. The rasping process will remove some of the periople from the wall of the foot. Hoof oil will help to protect the foot while the periople grows over the wall again.

f. The pritchel end of the buffer may be used for cleaning out nail holes; for example, when a used shoe is being reused and an old nail head may need removing.

g. The cost of a set of shoes will depend on various factors: type and size of shoes/stud holes/special shoes, and so on.

h. The foot wall grows at the rate of approximately 1–1.5 cm per month. The growth rate may accelerate; for example, if the horse has access to spring grass. Irregular rates of growth can be seen as "grass rings" on the wall of the hoof. More obvious and irregular rings or ridges of growth are most commonly an indication that the horse or pony has had laminitis.

i. Only attempt to remove a shoe yourself if it has slipped badly to one side and is in danger of harming the horse or if more damage will be done to the foot by leaving it. It is better to wait for the farrier. In the UK it is illegal for anyone who is not a registered farrier to shoe a horse or trim its feet.

Follow-up Work to Confirm Knowledge and Experience

1. Students taking the Stage Two examination must be able to show

how they would go about removing a shoe. If possible, ask your farrier to supervise you removing your own horse's shoe. Practise on both a front and a hind shoe as different techniques are used. This practice at practical application will prove invaluable as, however often you watch shoes being removed, it is never quite the same when you come to do it yourself.

2. Watch the farrier at work whenever possible, especially when different horses are being shod and if different shoes are being used. Make sure you know and understand each stage of the process.

3. Develop an eye for the well-shod horse by examining as many different shod horses as possible. Look at the wear on the shoes, the angle of the foot and pastern and the action of the horse.

4. Study the different tools available for use by the farrier to make sure you can recognise each one.

Helpful Hints and Exam Technique

 Carry a hoof pick in your pocket. When talking about shoeing and the horse's shoes, you will find it easier to take out your own hoof pick to pick out feet and examine the shoes rather than having to go in search of one. Don't forget to pick out feet into a skip to keep the yard and bed clean.

12 Health

1. Signs of the Horse Being in Good Health

a. The horse should be "well covered" or "well furnished". This means having enough muscle and fat on its body to cover its skeletal frame in such a way that there are no prominent bony areas.

b. The horse is alert, with ears mobile.

c. It is eating and drinking normally.

d. Salmon-pink mucous membranes.

e. Supple skin, moving easily over the body.

f. A shine to the coat.

g. No abnormal heat or swellings.

h. Droppings should break as they hit the ground, and be green or golden in colour depending upon the feed eaten. Horses pass droppings approximately ten to 15 times during a 24-hour period, depending upon the diet fed.

i. Urine should be pale yellow.

j. Normal temperature: 100–101°F or 38°C at rest.

k. Normal pulse 35–45 beats per minute; higher for foals, varying between 50–100 beats per minute at rest.

l. Normal respiration: 8–12 in-and-out breaths per minute at rest.

m. Able to carry its weight evenly on all four feet.

n. No sign of discharge from nose or eyes. Eyes fully open.

o. When a skin recoil test is made (that is, the skin on the neck is pinched

- A vet or horse dentist should visit and check teeth approximately twice a year. If a horse is very young or very old, such visits are especially necessary, as these are the times when most dentistry problems in horses occur

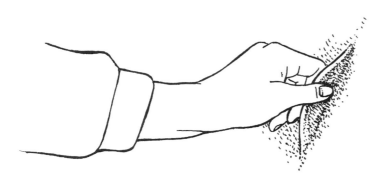

*Neck pinch, used in a
skin recoil test*

between thumb and first finger), the skin should recoil immediately, demonstrating its elasticity.

p. Normal response to capillary refill test. This is tested by pressing the gum with your thumb, which restricts the flow of blood. When you remove your thumb, the capillaries should immediately refill with blood.

2. Signs of the Horse Being Unwell

a. If any one, or all of these, is prominent: ribs/hips/croup/backbone, or if the top of the neck is sunken, then the horse is underweight.

b. Not alert, head low and ears unresponsive.

c. Not eating or drinking usual amounts.

d. Mucous membranes may be yellow (indicating jaundice and disruption of the liver), pale (indicating anaemia, probably due to infection) or blue (indicating lack of oxygen, due to poor circulation).

e. Skin appears taut. When the skin recoil test is made, the pinched skin stands proud, being slow to recoil.

f. The coat is dull and staring.

g. Abnormal areas of heat and swelling.

h. Droppings may be loose, very hard and/or irregular.

i. Urine red/brown or black.

j. Temperature, pulse and respiration (TPR) may be raised or lowered: temperature more than 1°F, or 0.5°C above or below normal. Pulse raised or lowered. Respiration shallow and rapid.

k. Showing unlevel steps.
l. Discharge from the nostrils or eyes.
m. Eyes not fully open and/or third eyelid showing.
n. Blood slow to return to capillaries after refill test.
o. Showing signs of discomfort. For example, pacing round the box, looking around at, or kicking at, belly; frequently getting up and lying down; pawing the ground; trying to stale and failing; patchy sweat; "tucked up".
p. Excessively overweight.

Finally, as each horse will have its own distinct habits and behaviour patterns, make sure you know your horse well. In this way you will notice the slightest abnormality that may indicate ill health. Act immediately if you notice something is amiss. Report to the yard manager or call the vet. Quick responses may limit the spread of disease, reduce the need for lengthy treatment and keep the horse's suffering to a minimum.

3. Preventive Measures

It is important to incorporate regular inspections into your daily routine. While working around the horses, you must constantly observe them. First thing in the morning, however, the horses will have been unobserved for many hours, therefore this first inspection is vital.

Check water supplies, rugs and signs of health, making sure the horses are safe, happy and healthy. The same applies before and after a lunch break and especially last thing at night when you must make every effort to ensure the horses are securely and safely rugged and stabled with a plentiful water supply. Do the same for your field-kept horses. In this way, many accidents and illnesses can be avoided.

• Report to the yard manager or call the vet if any worries arise regarding a horse's health. A quick response may limit the spread of disease, reduce the need for lengthy treatment, and keep the horse's suffering to a minimum

Apart from good general stable management, various types of routine health care are important in the prevention of ill health.

Worming

a. All horses carry a worm burden. However, an excessive amount will cause disruption of the digestive system, damage to internal organs and general ill health. If untreated, the horse may die.

b. Foals should start being wormed from six weeks of age.

c. To keep the worm burden low, horses should be "wormed" with a recognised brand of wormer on a regular basis. Worm every six to eight weeks if your horse is grazing with many other horses on infrequently rested pasture. Worm every six to eight weeks if your horse is stabled and/or grazing with few other horses on well-rested pasture that is also grazed by cattle/sheep.

d. Wormers are available in the form of powder/granules, paste and liquid. Different brands will destroy different species of worm. Some worms may become resistant to various brands so it is advisable to change your brand once or twice yearly. Ask your vet for advice.

Worming the horse

e. The wormer may be fed to the horse in its feed but many dislike the taste and refuse to eat it. Paste and liquid may be squirted directly into the horse's mouth by means of a large syringe. There is usually a guide to dosage on the syringe, which you preset before inserting it into the corner of the horse's mouth (where there are no teeth) then press the plunger, aiming the dose as far towards the back of the tongue as possible. It may be necessary to hold the horse's head up to prevent the dose dribbling or being spat out before the horse has swallowed.

f. There are three main types of wormers for horses, which are sold under a variety of different brand names. These wormers are benzimidazole, pyrantel and ivermectin.

g. The most common worms to invade the horse's system are: small redworm (small strongyles), large redworm (large strongyles), roundworm (ascarids), pinworm or seatworm, lungworm, bots and tapeworms.

h. Eggs of the small redworm pass out in the dung. They hatch to release larvae. Within a week the larvae develop if the conditions are warm and moist. Grazing horses ingest these larvae which burrow into the gut lining. From here they emerge as egg-laying adults so the life cycle is complete. They pose the greatest threat to the horse because of the damage they can do to the gut. During the summer some larvae develop into adults within six weeks but others remain in the gut wall throughout the autumn and winter. These are called encysted fourth-stage larvae. These larvae can emerge en masse in late winter and early spring, damaging the gut wall and causing colic, diarrhoea, weight loss and general unthriftiness. Not all wormers are effective against the encysted larvae. A five-day programme dosing with benzimidazole should be effective.

i. Eggs of the large redworm pass out in the dung. Larvae can hatch within three days and are eaten by grazing horses. The larvae penetrate the gut wall and migrate through the major arteries which supply blood to the gut. This can cause blood clots and blockages, cutting off blood supply to the gut. The larvae return to the gut and mature into adults. They attach to the intestinal lining and suck blood. At this point the females lay eggs. Large redworm are less of a problem now that modern

The standard to aim for. A horse in excellent health. Note the alert expression, shiny coat and the well-furnished body. There are no obvious signs of ailment or injury

wormers are better at controlling the larval stages. Ivermectin is effective against the migrating larvae and is most effectively given between October and December.

j. Roundworm eggs pass out in the droppings. The larvae develop within the egg in 10–14 days. The eggs are eaten by the grazing horses and hatch, then burrow through the wall of the intestine. They are carried by the circulatory system to the liver where they develop further. Eventually they migrate to the lungs and work their way through the blood vessels into the airways. They are then coughed up and swallowed, finally maturing into egg-laying adults in the small intestine. The eggs are very resistant to the effects of the weather. They are therefore able to survive and reinfect the horse easily. Foals are particularly prone to infestation which will cause coughing and generally poor growth and condition. Regular worming, combined with removing droppings from the field, is essential to control these worms.

k. Adult female pinworms lay their eggs when they emerge from the anus, on the surrounding skin. The larvae hatch. This makes the horse itch. An infected horse can be seen frequently scratching its tail by rubbing it against walls, fences, etc. The larvae are eaten by the horse, passing to the large intestine where they burrow into the lining and complete their development. Regular worming will control these parasites.

l. Lungworm larvae develop from the eggs passed out in the dung. They need warm, moist conditions to survive. Grazing horses swallow the larvae which burrow through the wall of the intestine and are carried through the bloodstream to the lungs. They break out into the air sacs and often fail to develop beyond this stage. If they do develop, the adults lay eggs which are coughed up, swallowed, then passed out in the droppings. They can cause damage, irritation and persistent coughing. Donkeys are the primary host for lungworm. Regular worming is essential.

m. Tapeworms do not affect all horses. In early summer a horse may ingest pasture mites when grazing. These mites may contain tapeworm larvae which will, in turn, infect the horse. A double dose of pyrantel in September is effective against tapeworm.

n. Gadflies pester horses during the summer and lay eggs which they "cement" to the horse's coat. Horses lick the emerging larvae which burrow into the mucous membrane of the gums and tongue. After about a month the larvae migrate to the stomach lining. They stay there until the following spring when they will detach themselves, pass out in the dung, burrow into the ground and pupate. Three to ten weeks later the adult fly emerges. Bots are therefore larvae of the gadfly, rather than worms. Ivermectin given in December is effective against bots which will have reached the stomach by this time in the year.

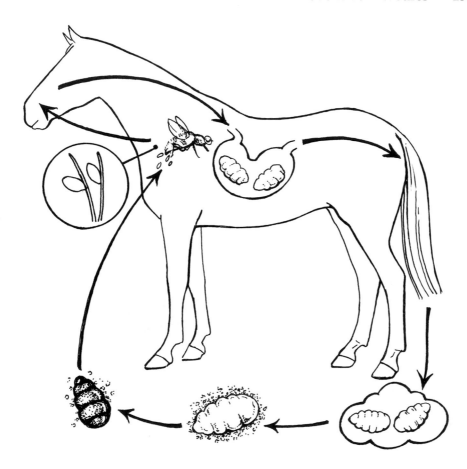

The life cycle of the gadfly

o. It is possible to have the effectiveness of your worming programme checked by taking a dung sample to a veterinary
laboratory for analysis. The egg count will reveal whether your
horse is carrying a normal worm burden or not.

Teeth

a. The horse's top jaw is wider than its bottom jaw. As the horse
masticates and its teeth wear down, sharp edges develop on the
outer edge of the upper set of molars and also on the inner edge

A vet, or horse dentist, should check the teeth of all the horses in a yard approximately twice a year. Where there are sharp edges on teeth, they should be rasped off. The effect of rasping teeth is shown here: (left) *before and* (right) *after*

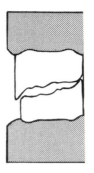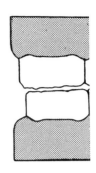

of the lower set. These sharp edges can cut into the horse's cheeks when it is eating or wearing tack. Some of the feed, especially hay and grass, may be partly chewed and then spat out because of the discomfort. This is called quidding. When ridden, the horse may resist the bit or drool from one side of its mouth.

b. A vet or horse dentist should visit and check teeth approximately twice a year. He or she will examine the mouth and rasp off sharp edges if necessary, as well as checking for loose, chipped or infected teeth. If sharp teeth are left unattended, the horse will suffer from poor digestion and loss of condition.

c. You can check for sharp teeth yourself by slipping your thumb up inside the horse's cheek and, taking care not to get nipped, feeling for sharp notches on the first couple of upper molars.

d. As well as checking the teeth, take time out to check inside your horse's mouth at least once per week. This out-of-sight area is often forgotten. With one arm and hand around the horse's nose to keep the horse's head still, use your other hand to part the lips gently so that you can examine the gums, tongue and visible teeth. Look carefully at the inner edge of the corners of the lips which sometimes crack and get sore if there is a bitting problem. Look also for bruising, sores and signs of teething or injury. If you slip your fingers in the side of the mouth where there are no teeth and gently push the tongue back a little, the horse will usually open its mouth. This is safer than trying to take the tongue out of the horse's mouth. If you are holding its tongue and the horse suddenly pulls away, it is possible for the tongue to be torn. While you are restraining the horse check that the curb groove is clean and free from sores, as sweat, saliva, etc., often collect here, particularly if the horse wears a drop noseband or similar item of tack.

Vaccinations

a. Tetanus is an essential vaccination for all horses. Pregnant mares should be given a booster injection in the last month of pregnancy to help to protect the newborn foal. A foal can then be vaccinated at around three months of age. Initially two injections are given four to six weeks apart, then a third injection one year later. After this, horses should be given a booster injection every two years.

b. Vaccination against equine influenza is not essential but it is advisable. For horses taking part in affiliated competitions, it is compulsory. An initial injection is given, followed by a booster four to six weeks later, then a third injection six months after that. The horse then needs to receive annual boosters. For competition purposes, rules state that the first two injections must be no less than 21 days apart and no more than 92 days. The third injection must then be given no less than 150 days after the second one and no more than 215 days. Subsequent boosters must be given no more than one year apart.

c. Flu and tetanus vaccinations are frequently given as a combined injection.

d. Other vaccinations may be given from time to time under certain circumstances. These will include: vaccination against equid herpesvirus 1 (rhinopneumonitis) for pregnant mares, and equine viral arteritis (EVA).

4. Heath Records

In order to keep track of the vet's visits, worming dates, etc., a record should be kept for each horse, perhaps in the form of a chart, including the dates of:

- Last worming dose, type of wormer used and date next wormer due.

Keeping a close check on the horse's health is essential practice. Here the horse is being wormed, part of a regular health routine

- When teeth were checked and next date due.
- When flu and tetanus vaccinations were given and when next due.
- When last shod and date of farrier's next visit.
- The vet's last visit and why he or she attended.

5. When to Call the Vet

a. If a wound is bleeding profusely, is more than skin deep, or is spurting blood (indicating a cut artery).
b. The horse exhibits any signs of colic.
c. The horse's temperature is more than one degree F higher or lower than normal.
d. If the horse is lame.
e. If the horse is coughing repeatedly and not clearing its nostrils after coughing.
f. If the horse is not responding in its usual way and generally seems off colour.
g. If in doubt, call the vet. It is better to be safe than sorry!
h. A horse suffering from any of the above conditions should not be worked. This may seem obvious but there have been cases where, for example, a horse has shown symptoms of mild colic which then appear to cease. The horse has been ridden soon after and had another colic attack with the rider on board; or a slightly lame horse has been ridden, the lameness appears to wear off but after work the horse has been much lamer than before. So, wait for veterinary advice.
i. If you think a wound may need to be stitched do not apply anything other than cold water as creams, powders and sprays will interfere with the healing process and may make the wound unstitchable.
j. When the vet arrives, he or she should be given the following information if possible and where relevant to the problem: how long the horse has had the complaint; recordings of TPR while the horse has been ill; what symptoms have been displayed; what action has been taken; how the injury occurred; if the horse has staled or passed droppings recently and were they normal;

whether the horse has any known disease/problems/allergies or allergic reactions to medication.

6. Minor Wounds

a. You can treat many minor wounds yourself, without veterinary assistance, provided that you have a first-aid kit, including:

  - hose and cold water supply
  - scissors
  - cotton wool
  - salt
  - warm water
  - clean bowl
  - wound powder/cream
  - antiseptic spray
  - gamgee
  - veterinary and stable bandages

b. Bruising is accompanied by heat and swelling. This can be effectively reduced by cold hosing, especially if the bruising is on the leg. To make sure you do not frighten the horse, start with a trickle of water and gradually move the trickle from the foot up the horse's leg to the damaged area. The water pressure can then be gradually increased. If there is an open wound with the bruising, hosing will help to remove the mud, etc., and clean the wound. Hose above an open wound, to allow the water to trickle over it. Do not hose directly on to an open wound.

c. Bleeding may be stopped by applying direct, firm pressure to the wound with a clean pad.

d. Once bleeding has ceased, any hair overlapping the wound should be carefully trimmed away. This will help you to see the extent of the wound.

e. Warm, salty water works as a safe and mild antiseptic with which you can clean the wound. (Prepare it by using 1 teaspoon of salt to $1/2$ litre/1 pt of boiled, then cooled, water.)

f. Dip cotton wool into the salty water and clean the wound, working from the middle outwards. Be careful not to rub grit into the wound and use a fresh piece of cotton wool for each wipe, never returning a dirty piece of cotton wool to the clean salt water, nor to the wound.

g. Dry the wound and then apply wound powder, spray or cream.

h. This procedure can be followed for all minor wounds, whether they be a saddle sore, scratch, kick, etc. Hosing can only really be used on the lower part of the body as higher up would involve soaking a large part of the horse, which would certainly be inappropriate in cold weather.

i. If the wound is within the mouth, clean by irrigation with salt water, and do not use a bit if it is likely to interfere, until the wound has healed. If the horse has a split in the corner of its lip, clean with salt water and then apply Vaseline.

7. Nursing a Sick Horse

a. The horse should have very frequent visits to check that there is no deterioration in its condition but visits should be made with a minimum of disturbance.

b. A regular check should be made and written records kept of its TPR and other general points to do with its condition; for example, how much it is eating, if there is more or less swelling, whether the horse is lying down more or less, etc.

c. Remove droppings frequently and keep the bed level, with good high banks. Short straw, or shavings, allow for ease of movement. Shavings will stick into wounds, however, and should be avoided for this type of ailment. Full mucking out may not be possible if the horse has limited movement. Use the deeper litter system in this case.

d. Keep the stable well ventilated but free from draughts.

e. Keep the horse warm but not weighed down with heavy clothing. Use leg bandages – and possibly a hood – to keep extremities warm. Use light, quilted rugs.

f. Do not groom vigorously if the horse is weak. Pick out the feet twice daily. Sponge eyes, nose and under the dock each day. Lightly brush over, being careful not to let the horse get cold.

g. If worn, remove bandages daily and hand massage the legs to improve the circulation.

h. Monitor the horse's water intake and keep the supply very fresh.

i.   Give light, tempting but laxative feeds. Remove any uneaten food immediately. Stale food and water will discourage the horse and possibly delay recovery.

j.   Follow veterinary instructions carefully.

k.   If the horse has an eye injury, keep the stable darkened and avoid bright lights.

l.   Unless the vet advises otherwise, give an ad lib supply of hay.

8. How to Recognise Lameness

a.   When lame in a front limb/foot, the horse will be reluctant to put its weight on the lame leg. In order to keep as much weight as possible off this leg, the horse will raise its head up as it puts this leg to the ground. When it puts its sound leg to the ground, it will put extra weight on it and drop its head down as it does so.

b.   Walking straight towards you, on firm, level ground, you may observe the head and neck of the sound horse bobbing gently in rhythm with the walk. Trotting straight towards you, the head and neck of the sound horse will be held level.

c.   If you watch the head and neck of a horse that is lame in a front limb, in either walk or trot, you will notice it raise its head high when the lame leg comes to the ground and drop its head low when the sound leg comes to the ground.

d.   The extent to which the horse raises and lowers its head will depend upon the degree of lameness, varying from a slight nod to a very pronounced movement up and down.

e.   Hind leg lameness can be more difficult to detect. Watching a sound horse from behind, the hindquarters should rise and fall evenly as the horse walks or trots away from you on a straight line.

f.   A horse that is lame behind will drop one quarter lower and raise one quarter higher. This may be difficult to see if the lameness is only slight.

Follow-up Work to Confirm Knowledge and Experience

1.   To gain experience in all matters to do with the horse's health, it is essential to have worked with a large number of horses and

ponies. Until you have actually seen a variety of diseases/wounds and have been involved in treating and nursing these horses, you cannot be completely aware of the problems involved and the signs to look for. Each horse or pony will react a little differently and the circumstances in which the horses are kept will have a bearing on how each problem is tackled.

Helpful Hints and Exam Technique

 The subject of health may come up in various different parts of the exam, both when working with the horse and during theoretical discussion. Some candidates make the mistake of forgetting the obvious with this topic. The examiner is usually looking for basic practical answers, not complicated veterinary knowledge which is best left to the vets themselves.

13 The Horse's Digestive System

Through knowledge of the digestive system, we can become more aware of problems when feeding horses and therefore improve feeding management.

1. General Outline of the Digestive System

a. Lips – gather the food.

b. Teeth – The incisors (at the front) are the cutters. The molars (at the back) then grind the food down so that it can be swallowed.

c. Tongue – Moves the food from the front to the back and sides of the mouth and then forms a portion of food into a bolus ready for swallowing.

d. Salivary glands – Saliva is discharged into the mouth through tiny openings. While making the food wet and warm, it also contains enzymes that help to break it down.

e. Epiglottis – Blocks the entrance to the trachea to ensure that food passes down the oesophagus only, not into the lungs.

f. Oesophagus – Also called the gullet, this is the tube that leads to the stomach. Up to 1.5 m (5 ft) in length, it runs from the throat down the neck, through the chest between the lungs, then through the diaphragm into the stomach.

g. Stomach – Approximately the size of a rugby ball but expands to accommodate 9–18 litres (2–4$^1/_2$ gal). A muscle called the cardiac sphincter controls the outlet. Gastric juice, containing enzymes and acid, is added in the stomach, to aid the digestion of the food.

h. Small intestine – Formed of three parts. First, the duodenum, 1 m (39 in) in length; then the jejunum, 20 m (66 ft) long; finally, the ileum, 2 m (6$^1/_2$ ft) long. All together, these three parts can hold

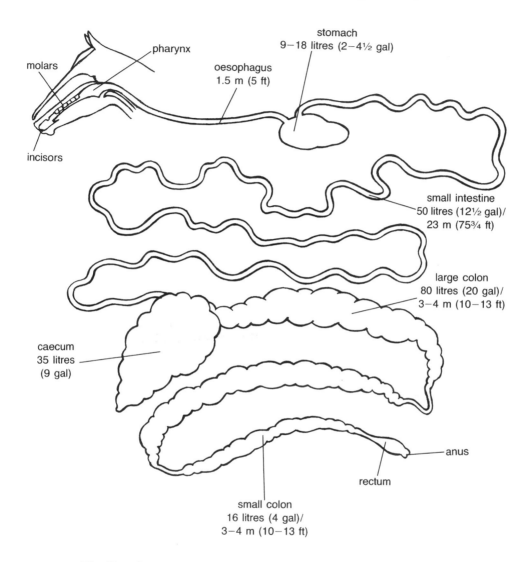

The digestive system

approximately 50 litres (12^1/$_2$ gal). Fluids from the liver and pancreas are secreted into the small intestine to break down the food, while some nutrients are absorbed into the bloodstream. Muscular contractions, called peristalsis, move the food along.

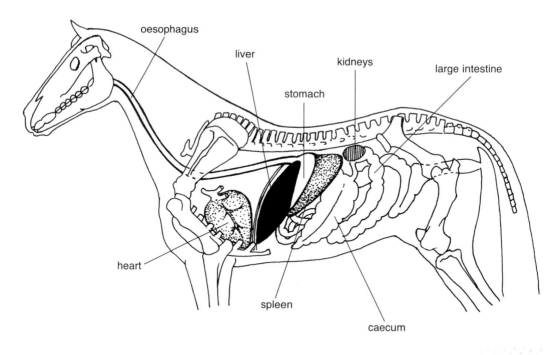

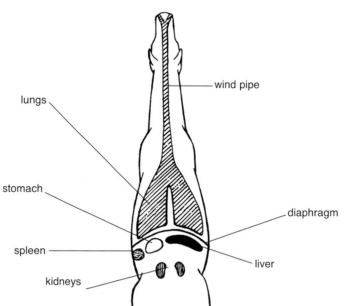

The position of the main internal organs

i. Large intestine – This starts with the caecum, which holds about 35 litres (9 gal) and acts as a holding chamber for the next section, which is called the large or great colon. The great colon is 3–4 m (10–13 ft) long and holds up to 80 litres (20 gal). From these sections, water is absorbed, while bacteria break down the cellulose part of the food. This breakdown may take several days. The next section is the small colon, where nutrients and water are also extracted. It is 3–4 m (10–13 ft) long but only holds up to 16 litres (4 gal). The small colon ends in the rectum, where the waste material is formed into dung which then passes out through the anus.

2. Additional Information

a. Teeth – The molars, which are used to grind up the food, wear against each other. As the upper jaw is wider than the lower one, the wear is often uneven. The horse may cease to chew properly, due to discomfort, which, in turn, may lead to digestive problems, coughing and resistance when being ridden.

b. The digestive tract, from lips to anus, is called the alimentary canal.

c. The liver and pancreas are accessory organs which aid digestion. The liver has many functions, one of them being to secrete bile which helps the horse to digest fat. The pancreas secretes digestive juices.

d. The horse's diet contains a large amount of cellulose, which is found in many feeds, especially grass. Cellulose is not broken down until it reaches the large intestine. This means that the food passing through the small intestine is still quite bulky.

e. From the food that horses eat, carbohydrates are broken down into sugars

- Food can take three to four days to pass right through the horse. This should be borne in mind if any changes are made to a horse's diet. A close check must be kept on the horse for several days to observe whether or not the change of diet has had any adverse effects

and used for energy; fats and oils (lipids) are broken down into fatty acids and glycerol; proteins are broken down into amino acids and used for body building.

f. It takes approximately 24 hours for the horse to empty a full stomach but it is better for the stomach to be just half-full most of the time.

g. Food can take three to four days to pass right through the horse.

h. The cardiac sphincter muscle acts as a one-way valve which prevents the regurgitation of food.

i. The great colon is so long that it folds back on itself. It also narrows at one of the bends, which makes it prone to blockages.

j. You can see food passing down the oesophagus on the left side of the horse's neck behind the trachea.

Follow-up Work to Confirm Knowledge and Experience

1. It can be difficult to remember the various parts of a system when it is not possible to see it. Try building a model to which you can relate visually to help you to remember the system. Use any props available to construct a mock digestive system. Hose pipes, buckets, string, a football – all could be used to give visual meaning to the lengths and capacities mentioned. For example, measure out litres of water to show the stomach's capacity; measure a length of hose to show how long the small intestine is; and use a feed sack to represent the caecum.

2. Practise saying the unfamiliar words aloud, until you are comfortable with them. Find someone who can listen to and check your pronunciation.

3. Use word association to help you to remember words which are particularly difficult for you. For example, if you find it hard to remember the incisors, think of scissors for cutting, which is a similar-sounding word and an instrument which does the same cutting job as the incisor teeth.

Helpful Hints and Exam Technique

Try not to become flustered if you forget the names of various parts of the system under the pressure of the exam situation. The examiner will give you time to think and come back to a point you have problems with.

Try to learn the basic system and avoid confusing your memory with too many extra details. Don't worry if other candidates come out with details you don't know about, as they have probably managed to learn much more than they need to know for the exam.

14 The Skeleton

1. Why We Need to Know about the Skeleton

a. By learning where the bones are located, we can avoid causing damage to the horse; for example, when wisping, it is important to avoid bony areas.
b. If a horse receives an injury, we will know if that location may have involved a bone. This will help when deciding whether or not to call the vet.
c. Understanding the structure of the horse helps in the assessment of conformation, which, in turn, helps us to understand each horse's limitations.

2. Aspects of Note

a. The skeleton is the structure or framework around which the body is built.
b. When the joints are used, the skeleton is mobile rather than rigid.
c. There are three types of joint:

- Immovable joints – where bones fuse together, like those in the skull.
- Slightly movable joints – where bones are not fused together but movement is very limited, as in the backbone.
- Freely movable joints – these divide into a further four types: plane, hinged, pivot, and ball and socket.

d. The skull protects the brain and parts of the ears, eyes and nasal passages. Along with the lower jaw bone, it also houses the teeth.
e. The bones of the backbone are called vertebrae. There is a channel running through these vertebrae. The spinal cord runs along this channel and is protected by it.
f. The five sacral vertebrae are fused together.

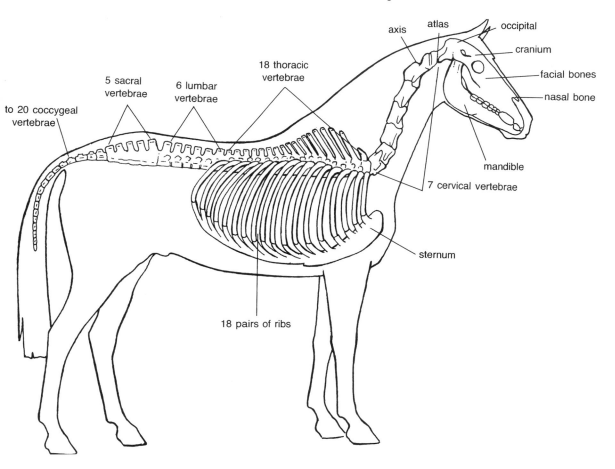

Axial skeleton (bones of the skull, spine, ribs and sternum)

g. The 18 pairs of ribs, which are attached to the thoracic vertebrae, protect many of the internal organs, especially the lungs.

h. Eight pairs of ribs are "true" ribs and ten pairs are "false". The "true" pairs attach directly to the sternum as well as to the vertebrae, while the "false" pairs are attached to the vertebrae but are only attached to the sternum by cartilage.

i. The front limbs have no bony attachment to the rest of the skeleton. They are only joined by muscles, tendons and ligaments. (The horse does not have a collar bone.)

j. The pelvis is formed by a number of fused bones: the fused sacral

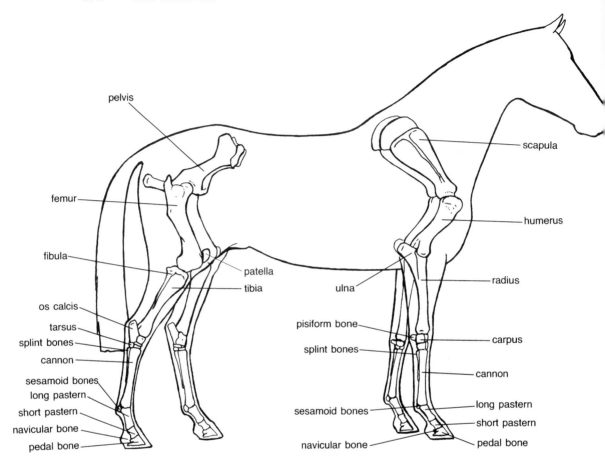

Appendicular skeleton (bones of the limbs)

vertebrae, ilium, pubis and ischium.

k. Some bones contain marrow, which is where blood cells are formed.

l. Cartilage is a smooth, flexible substance. While the horse is still growing, it can be found at the ends of long bones, where it ossifies into bone. It is also found

- The skeleton is the framework around which the body is built and therefore provides the structure to which the muscles are attached. This fact should be kept in mind when checking the horse for injury

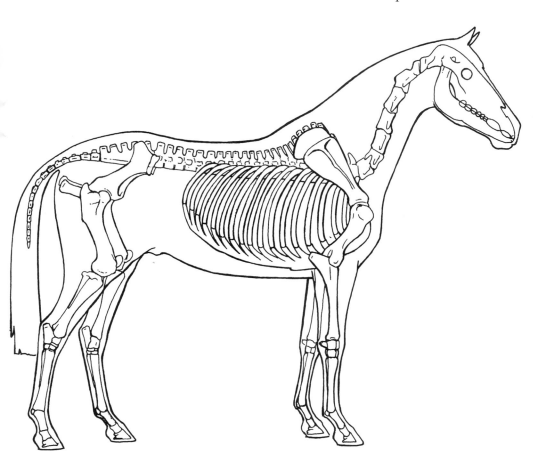

The whole skeleton

in joints, where, by covering the surfaces of the bones that meet, it prevents friction. Being flexible, it can help to give support, while allowing for movement; for example, the rings of cartilage in the trachea and the cartilage that joins some of the ribs to the sternum.

- Many bones have surface projections that aid the attachment of muscles; for example, the spinal processes of the vertebrae

m. Many bones have surface projections that aid the attachment of muscles; for example, the spinal processes of the vertebrae.

n. If we imagine the human as an animal on all fours, we can see that many of the horse's joints are equivalent to our own.

- horse's stifle – human knee
- horse's hock – human heel
- horse's knee – human wrist
- horse's leg below the knee – human middle finger

Follow-up Work to Confirm Knowledge and Experience

1. Having studied a picture of the skeleton, it is vital for the student to take the picture and look at it in conjunction with a real horse standing in front of them. It is easy to fall into the trap of being familiar with the picture but not being able to relate it to the live horse.

2. It is also a good idea to take any opportunity to study the horse in motion and look at how the skeleton is moved, noting the different types of joints at the same time.

Helpful Hints and Exam Technique

 If you have difficulty remembering where bones and joints are under exam conditions, it is sometimes helpful to lift one of the horse's limbs, which helps you to see where the joints are.

 If you cannot remember some of the names of bones, at least make sure you can point out approximately where each bone starts and finishes.

15 Aspects of Yard Management

1. Safety

Clothing for Working around Horses

a. Strong footwear, to protect you if trodden on, etc., is essential. The ideal would be boots with steel toe caps which are now more readily available. Leather boots give good protection. The soles must provide good grip.

b. All clothing must allow freedom of movement. However, if too loose and baggy, it can catch on things or flap and frighten the horse.

c. Bright colours may be frightening. If worn, the wearer should be aware of introducing them gradually to their horses.

d. Gloves should be worn whenever possible. By preventing wounds and scratches on your hands, you avoid problems like tetanus and Weil's disease.

e. All jewellery should be avoided. Rings, bracelets, earrings, etc., can easily get caught up and cause serious injury to the wearer.

f. Long hair can also get caught and is better tied back or worn under a hat.

g. A hard hat should be worn when handling problem or young horses.

h. For riding, a hard hat of Standard PAS 015 or EN1384 must always be worn. Footwear must have a small block heel, not a wedge type, to prevent the foot from slipping through the stirrup and becoming stuck. The sole should be fairly smooth, as deep ridges may also cause feet to get stuck.

General Safety around the Yard

Keeping the yard tidy is the most important step towards safety. Any item left lying around can become a hazard. The tidying up process is usually called "setting fair".

a. A bag or bin can be provided for any string removed from hay and straw bales.

b. Yard tools need hooks to hang from or a specific storage room.

c. The yard surface should be non-slip and kept free from debris by regular sweeping. This will also remove loose hay and straw that could become a fire hazard.

d. Grooming kit, tack, clothing, buckets, etc., must always be put away. Hay nets pose a particular hazard for both horse and human if left lying around.

e. When a full hay net is given to a horse, it should be tied up bearing in mind how low it will hang when empty. Pull the hay net up as high as possible, then draw the string through the bottom of the hay net and pull it back up to the top. Tie with a quick-release knot, then turn the net so that the knot is hidden at the back where it is less likely to be pulled undone by the horse.

f. Yard work often involves moving heavy objects. This can be hazardous if not tackled correctly. Always enlist the help of a fellow worker where possible. Trolleys, wheelbarrows, etc., should be used to move hay bales, feed sacks and other items, rather than trying to carry them.

g. When lifting, try to keep your back straight. Bend your knees rather than bending at the waist and push up using your thigh muscles, rather than pulling up with your back muscles.

h. Keep weights balanced; for example, carry two water buckets, one in each hand, rather than one on its own which will pull you sideways.

i. Carry heavy weights close to your body to help you to maintain balance.

j. General maintenance is essential. For example, door bolts need to work smoothly; electrical fittings must be secure and well insulated; holes in the yard or buildings need quick repair, and so on.

Further Points on Safety for Winter Weather Conditions

a. Do not empty water buckets, or run a hose, directly on to the yard as the water may freeze and cause a hazardous surface.

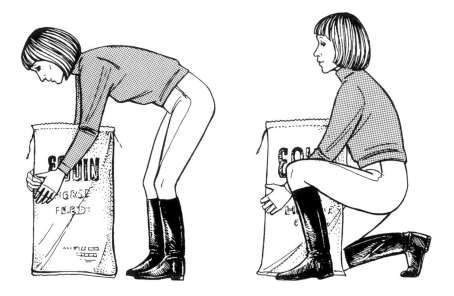

Lifting a heavy weight: the incorrect way (left) *and the correct way* (right)

b. Grit or salt can be spread over icy patches to maintain a safe surface.

c. Check drains and gutters more frequently as any blockage will quickly cause flooding in very wet weather.

d. Automatic water systems may need to be switched off and drained to prevent freezing and subsequent burst pipes.

e. Be aware that stabled horses often become more lively and difficult to handle in cold, windy weather. It may be necessary to lead a horse in its bridle for more control, even though you may normally lead it out on its head collar.

f. When riding out, be aware of slippery surfaces and previously muddy ground frozen into hard ruts. These hazardous surfaces may cause a fall and injury if not tackled with extra care.

g. Check field water troughs several times a day to break ice. Some self-filling troughs may not refill if pipes freeze, so check the water level.

h. Shorter, dark days mean that you frequently have to work in the dark, while power cuts are more likely in stormy weather. Try to prioritise and carry out essential jobs in the daylight. Make sure you know where to locate the trip switches, and keep plenty of torches to hand.

> • When riding out, be aware of slippery surfaces and previously muddy ground frozen into hard ruts. Such ground becomes very hazardous and the unevenness of the surface can cause horses to strain joints and tendons

Fire Precautions

a. Prevention is best so keep the yard tidy (as mentioned above) to prevent the spread of fire if it occurs.

b. A muck heap can get very hot and may self-ignite, so position it well away from buildings.

c. Hay, straw and shavings should be stored away from the stables.

d. Taps, hoses and troughs (keep them full) can all be used to fight a fire.

e. Arrange for a fire officer to visit. He or she will advise on fire extinguishers, telling you how many are needed, where to put them and what type to have.

f. Put up one or more fire notices. These should have white lettering on a green background and read as follows:

> IN THE EVENT OF A FIRE
> 1. Raise the alarm.
> 2. Move horses to safety.
> 3. Dial 999 for the fire brigade.
> 4. Fight the fire.

After each point, details are required:

- The location of the fire alarm.
- Designated place of safety for the horses.
- Location of the nearest telephone.
- Location of fire fighting equipment.

g. Put NO SMOKING notices around the yard and provide buckets full of sand in which cigarettes can be extinguished.

h. All workers should know and practise the yard fire drill.

Riding Out and the Country Code

There are various rules of safe conduct which help to maintain a good relationship between riders and other countryside users.

a. If on horseback when passing walkers or other riders, always walk and give them a wide berth. If you approach them from the rear, make your presence known. It is, in any case, only polite to say "Good morning", etc.

b. Do not ride on private land without permission. Keep to bridle-ways and other areas designated for horses.

c. Ride around the edges of fields with crops in them.

d. Do not ride through livestock. Walk around them, giving them a wide berth.

e. Leave gates as you find them, unless it is obvious that someone has forgotten to secure a gate and livestock are escaping, in which case inform the farmer.

f. Be aware of people, dogs, etc., in gardens. When hidden from your horse's view, behind a hedge or fence, any noise or movement could cause your horse to shy into the road.

g. Never trot around blind corners on roads or tracks. There could be any number of unforeseen hazards, so be prepared and slow to a walk.

h. Avoid busy roads where possible, and take the Riding and Road Safety Test.

2. Accident Procedure and Reports

It is advisable for everyone to have first-aid training, whatever their occupation. The following is the procedure to take in the event of an accident, rather than how to administer first aid.

Accident Procedure

a. First, remain calm as it is important to think clearly.

b. While the injured person is your first priority, you must make the situation safe while you make your way to them. If someone has been kicked, move the horse away. If someone has fallen off, halt the rest of the ride and send a responsible person to catch the loose horse. Each situation will be a little different, so use common sense.

c. Go to the injured person. Reassure them and tell them to keep still.

If Conscious

d. Encourage them to breathe deeply and calmly. (They may be winded and panicking about getting air.)

e. Ask them if there is any pain. Can they move their fingers and toes?

f. Make a mental note of what they say; it will be helpful information to give the doctor or ambulance staff, should they be needed.

g. Keep talking to the person. If they appear to be talking nonsense, they may have concussion and will need to be taken to a doctor.

h. If they cannot move their fingers or toes or have pain in the neck, back or limbs, do not move them. Ask for an ambulance to be called. Keep them warm with a blanket or jackets. Do not try to remove hat or boots, etc.

i. Obvious bleeding should be stemmed by applying direct pressure with a handkerchief or clean pad.

j. If they feel fine and want to get up, allow them to do so on their own. Stand near in case they feel faint and need support. Do not allow them to remount if you feel there is any chance they may faint, or if they have hit their head.

k. Allow them to walk for a while before remounting, and continue with an easy, confidence-giving exercise, or let them sit quietly before resuming their work which should be of an undemanding nature.

If Unconscious

l. Check that there is no blockage in the mouth that may prevent breathing and carefully loosen any tight clothing around the neck.

m. Do not move the person unless they are in danger of choking and need their airway kept clear by putting them in the recovery position (this should be done with great care to keep the spine straight). Send for an ambulance. Anyone who has been unconscious must be examined by a doctor in case of skull damage.

n. Keep talking to them; this may help to bring them round. Keep them warm.

o. Remain calm and also reassure the rest of your ride as soon as possible. Once the injured person has been taken to hospital, you may resume the work, hack or lesson.

Further Points

a. Be prepared for accidents. Have the telephone number of your local doctor and vet clearly displayed by the telephone. Dial 999 for an ambulance. Have a human first-aid kit on the yard and also one that can be taken out when hacking.

b. If you have a pay phone, keep money for emergencies in an obvious place beside the phone. When hacking, take money for the phone.

c. If an accident occurs on the road, someone should be posted on each side of an injured person to redirect traffic around them. With luck, there will be a motorist with a mobile phone or you may have a mobile phone with you with which to summon help. It is obviously important to catch the loose horse as it may cause further accidents. On return home you should fill in a British Horse Society accident report form. This helps the Road Safety Development Officer of the BHS to compile statistics on road accidents involving horses.

d. If an accident involves injury to human and horse, take care of the human first but attend to the horse or send someone else to do so as soon as possible.

Accident and Incident Reports

a. In all yards an accident book should always be kept in which all incidents and accidents are recorded. You could have two books, one for minor incidents and one for more serious accidents.

b. Records should include: date, place and time of incident, name of person or persons involved and what they were doing at the time, what happened, what injuries (if any) were sustained, what horses (if any) were involved, whether the person was taken to hospital/doctor/home, etc. It is also a good idea to draw a sketch of the incident. For example, the position of jumps and other riders when a person fell off during a lesson.

• Make a mental note of anything that an injured person says; it will be helpful information to give the doctor or ambulance staff, should they be needed

c. When possible, any one who has witnessed an accident should be asked to sign the report.

d. The accident book should be available for staff and clients to look at if they wish and should therefore be kept in an accessible place in the office or similar room.

3. Stable Construction and Maintenance of Facilities

Site

a. If you are able to choose the site, the stables should be positioned with their backs to the prevailing wind.

b. Choose an area that should drain well. If at the bottom of a dip, the stables and drains may flood in wet weather.

c. Large trees too close to the building may pose a problem in stormy weather if a branch or the whole tree falls.

d. Other considerations include accessibility for vehicles, electricity and water.

Drainage and Flooring

a. Drains are generally laid to take all water away from the stables towards the rear.

b. When the floor is laid, a slight slope towards the front or rear is incorporated to aid drainage. If the slope drains into a front channel it is visible and easy to keep clear. However, as horses often stand at the front of their boxes, this may lead to them standing in the wettest area. If the slope drains into a back channel, it will be less visible and may become blocked but the horse will usually be standing in a drier area. Each individual must weigh up the pros and cons.

c. Drainage channels and covers must be swept clean daily.

d. Concrete, with little ridges on the surface for grip, is the most commonly used flooring. The concrete is laid some 1 m (3 ft) or so wider than the actual floor area needed. This allows for hard dry-standing immediately outside the boxes.

Walls

a. Wooden walls are frequently used and can be purchased in sections ready to erect.

b. Brickwork, one or two bricks high (or more), is put down as a base for the wooden structure. This helps to prevent rotting and invasion by vermin.

c. The higher the brick base, the more expensive the structure becomes. For this reason, complete brick-built boxes are not often erected these days.

d. Breeze blocks are a cheaper alternative and may be used as a compromise between brick and wood. The advantages of brick/breeze block over wood are that they are more durable and also fireproof.

e. A small hole must be incorporated in the base of the wall for drainage.

f. Walls should be approximately 240 cm (nearly 8 ft) high to the eaves to allow for head room.

g. Walls and doors need to be lined with kicking boards. This will protect both the outer walls and the horse from each other. Kicking boards also provide insulation and strengthen the walls. They are usually 120 cm (4 ft) high.

Dimensions

a. A box of 300 x 300 cm (10 x 10 ft) would provide enough room for a pony up to 14.2 h.h.

b. 300 x 360 cm (10 x 12 ft) or 360 x 360 cm (12 x 12 ft) provides enough room for a 14.2–16 h.h. horse.

c. 360 x 420 cm (12 x 14 ft) or 420 x 420 cm (14 x 14 ft) would be a suitable size for a horse 16.2 h.h. or over.
d. Boxes for very large horses, or for foaling, should be 480 x 480 cm (16 x 16 ft).
e. Doorways should be 120 cm (4 ft) wide, with a bottom-door height suitable for the size of horse. Horses of 14.2 h.h. and above will usually have a bottom door 120 cm (4 ft) high, with a top door of 90 cm (3 ft), making a total doorway height of 210 cm (7 ft).
f. Pony boxes will have lower bottom doors and will not require as much head room in the doorway.

Roof

a. A pitched roof gives more head room and air space inside the box and also drains well.
b. The roof should overhang the front of the boxes by approximately 90 cm to 1 m (about 3 ft). This will keep the horses dry and give shade when they have their heads over the door.
c. Air vents may be put in the roof to aid good circulation of air.
d. Roofing felt provides an attractive and relatively inexpensive roof covering. However, its insulation properties are poor and it is not fireproof. As it is inclined to expand and contract in hot and cold weather, cracks will gradually appear, leading to leaks.
e. Slate is more expensive, but it is attractive, insulates well and is fireproof. However, it does crack easily.
f. Tiles are more expensive still, but are strong, attractive and have excellent insulation properties which keep the stables warm in winter and cool in summer. They are also fireproof.
g. Corrugated sheets of plastic, iron, onduline and other modern materials can provide a cheaper form of roofing. Iron is the worst of these, being hot in summer, cold in winter and very noisy when it rains. Plastic is a useful addition to all types of roof as it provides an extra source of light. The other materials are fireproof and provide reasonable insulation. Cheap roofing is quick to erect but whole sheets will need replacing if damaged.

Fittings

a. Stable doors, particularly the top door which is rarely closed, need hooks to secure them when open.

b. When closed, they need strong bolts to secure them. On the bottom door use a bolt design that your horse cannot open at the top and a kick bolt at the bottom.

c. A metal strip along the top of the lower door can prevent the horse from chewing the wood. The upper part of the door frame may also be covered with metal to prevent chewing.

d. Windows should be located on the same side of the box as the door. This prevents through draughts, while providing light and fresh air.

e. Windows that hinge at the bottom to open outwards prevent draughts. They should be covered with wire mesh and be glazed with wired safety glass.

f. Louvre boards can provide further draught-free ventilation, and are usually positioned fairly high up on the wall.

A kick bolt secures the door and is quick and easy to use

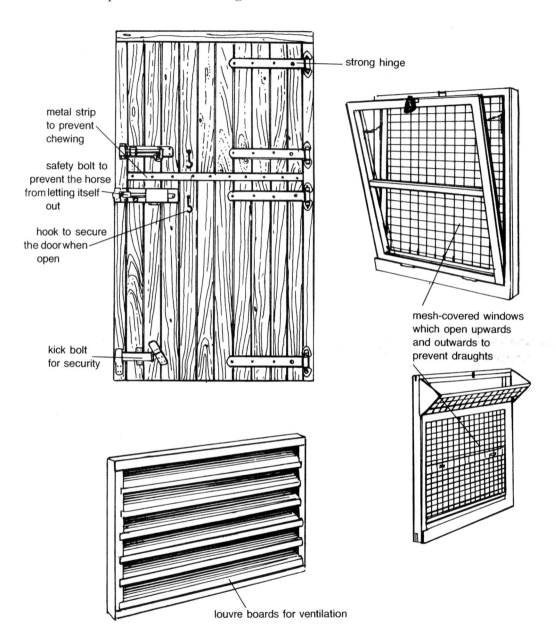

strong hinge

metal strip
to prevent
chewing

safety bolt to
prevent the horse
from letting itself
out

hook to secure
the door when
open

kick bolt
for security

mesh-covered windows
which open upwards
and outwards to
prevent draughts

louvre boards for ventilation

Safe stable fittings

g. Tie-up rings should be positioned towards the front of the box. Then, when the horse is tied up, you will be able to enter the box with the horse's head towards you, rather than its hindquarters. Fix the ring approximately at horse's eye level.

h. Further fittings, such as automatic water bowl, hay rack, feed manger, are optional. If used, there should be no sharp edges and each item should be high enough to prevent the horse from getting its legs caught.

i. Strip lighting or bulbs can be used. Position these well above the horse's head height. They must also be covered to prevent shattered glass from falling into the bed. The light switch should be outside the stable, out of the horse's reach. Obviously, all electrical wires must be well insulated and covered to keep them away from horses and protected from weather and rodent damage.

Converted Buildings

Many buildings are converted from their original use for use as stables. It is important to check that these conversions will provide a safe environment for the horse. Each situation will vary but the following points should be considered.

a. Buildings and dividing walls must be strong enough to withstand being kicked and leant on by the horse. Badly-built walls crumble and fall easily, while flimsy wood panels will splinter.

b. There must always be plenty of head room in the doorway and inside the building. Old barns with low beams may not be suitable.

c. Dividing walls that do not reach up to the ceiling must be high enough to stop the horse from fighting with its neighbours. Bars could be used so that the horses can still talk to each other.

d. Check that there are no protrusions that could damage the horse; for example, old nails, hooks, etc.

4. Knowledge of the British Horse Society (BHS)

As all candidates for the BHS examinations must be BHS members, it is important to understand the aims and objectives of the society, along with how it benefits them and others (not just examination candidates) to be a member.

The BHS is the lead body for the leisure riding public of the UK. It is also the governing body for professionals who teach in the horse industry. It is a membership organisation whose specific aims are:

- To improve the general standard of horse and pony welfare in Great Britain.
- To improve awareness of the horse generally.
- To improve the standard of equitation and horse knowledge amongst all sectors of the riding and carriage-driving public.
- To provide benefits for Society members.
- To improve access to the countryside for both the riding and driving public.

Benefits of BHS membership

1. Free publications giving information and advice on a wide variety of topics.
2. Membership facilities at major events.
3. Free personal liability and personal accident insurance.
4. Legal, tax, and rating helplines.

The Structure of the BHS

The national structure of the BHS consists of committees at country, regional, and county level. Each committee is made up of elected and appointed volunteers. Nine regional development officers, who are employees of the Society, support the volunteers.

The departments within the Society include: Access and Rights of Way; Welfare and Breeding; Riding Clubs; Safety Training and Education; Riding Schools and Recreational Riding; and Examinations.

Follow-up Work to Confirm Knowledge and Experience

1. Through working in an equestrian establishment, it should be possible for any student to observe how important safe working procedures are. Unfortunately, accidents will happen but it is hoped that each individual will learn by their mistakes.

2. Students at all levels should train themselves to ask the questions "Why?", "How?", "What is it?" and so on. They need to know about everything that goes on around them. In this way students will learn more and have a much deeper understanding of all aspects of yard work and management.

Helpful Hints and Exam Technique

 The subjects of safety, accident procedure and knowledge of the BHS will be examined at all levels. Candidates must show a really thorough knowledge of safety and accident procedure if an examiner is going to have confidence in their ability to work safely and sensibly with horses. While the candidate is unlikely to fail an exam due to lack of knowledge of the BHS, it does not give a very good impression if a person is a member of a society about which they know nothing! For your own sake, read the members' yearbook and see what you can gain from the BHS, rather than just being a member for the sake of your exams.

 When you are talking about routine, communications, records and stable construction, do use examples from your own experience. Describing methods or designs that you have seen in use, and highlighting both good and bad points, will immediately show the examiner that you really have been involved in working in a yard and therefore you have the practical experience which is so important.

16 Preparing to Take the Exam

1. Location

a. Once you know where you will be taking the exam it is a good idea to make a visit to the centre if it is not where you are already training.

b. By making a visit you can check your route and find out how long it will take you to get there.

c. On arrival introduce yourself and you will probably find some-one only too happy to show you round.

d. You are bound to feel more confident if you know where you are going and what you will find when you arrive.

e. You can also explore local facilities for lunch, or make plans to take sandwiches and drinks with you.

f. Do try to arrange for someone to go with you for the day. It is not a good idea to drive yourself when your mind is occupied with thoughts of the exam.

2. Clothing

a. A smart and practical turn out will immediately make a good impression. For the "Horse Knowledge and Care" section of the exam you need to feel comfort-able and able to work easily around the horses.

b. Have your hair tied back if it

- The general impression you make will go a long way towards making the final result a positive one. So try to be helpful and enthusiastic!

Suitable clothing for taking the exam: (left) *for riding and* (centre and right) *for stable management tasks depending on the weather conditions*

is long. Wearing a cap is quite acceptable if you feel comfortable doing so, but it is not essential.

c. You will probably be wearing a shirt and tie for the riding section of the exam. Cover this with a plain sweatshirt or jumper in cold weather, or just wear shirt and tie if very warm weather. On colder and wet days a waterproof coat that is not too big and bulky is acceptable.

d. If riding, a short "jumping" length whip is carried for the jumping section of the exam. A long whip may be carried for the general riding on the flat.

e. Jodhpurs are easy to work in and should be cream or beige if you

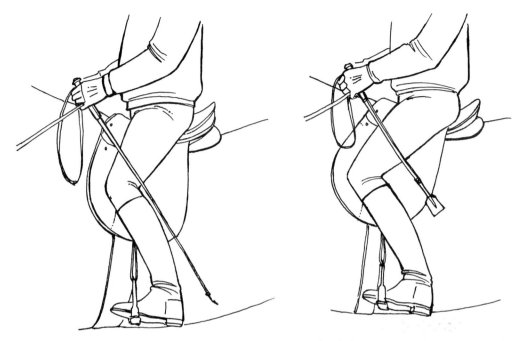

Whips: (left) *a long whip, for work on the flat and* (right) *a short whip for jumping*

are taking the riding section of the exam. If you are only taking the "Horse Knowledge and Care" section you could wear dark-coloured jodhpurs.

f. Good strong footwear is essential. Long riding boots can be restrictive to work in, but are perfectly acceptable if you are comfortable in them. Otherwise jodhpur boots are a smart and practical alternative. Make sure your boots are clean.

g. Take gloves with you for leading horses out of the stable.

3. Performance

a. Remember that examiners are watching you all the time. They are not just looking to see how you carry out the task set. They are looking at your general attitude to your work and the horses. Do you go about your work quickly? Are you confident and caring with the horses? Do you work in a tidy manner; skip up as you go along, and keep equipment organised?

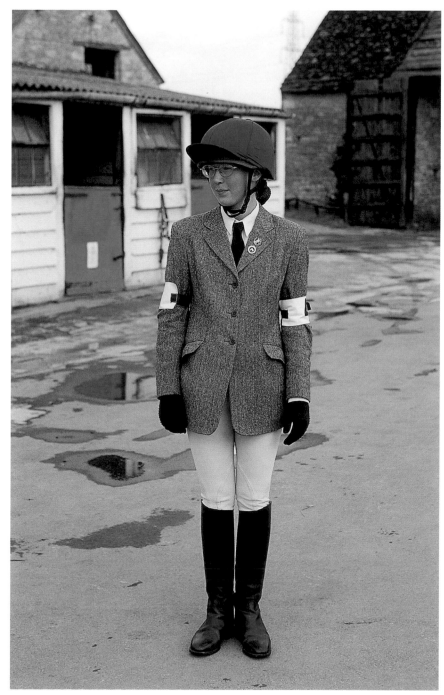

*A neat
and
practical
turnout
for the
riding
section of
an exam*

**This
photograph
was taken
under
examination
conditions at
The Talland
School of
Equitation**

b. The general impression you make will go a long way towards making the final result a positive one. So try to be helpful and enthusiastic.
c. It is important to be physically as fit as you can be when working with horses. If you work with horses on a daily basis, mucking out, sweeping yards, etc., and pay attention to correct lifting techniques and working procedures you will keep yourself fit and be able to perform to a higher standard both when riding and carrying out yard tasks.

If you are well prepared for this exam and don't rush into it you should find that you enjoy the day. Good luck.

Index

Note: page numbers in *italics* refer to illustrations